C000124972

The Beginner's Guide for Stress Management and Anxiety Relief

Stop Anxiety Now and Transform Your Life
Through the Power of Stress Management

Michael Robertson

TABLE OF CONTENTS

Introduction

You might be a parent caring for children. Maybe you're newly pregnant, or mired in a complex divorce. Perhaps you have just graduated from university and are wondering how you're ever going to pay off your student debt. Anxiety, heaviness in the chest, racing thoughts, and other symptoms of stress can be triggered by any major life event. Money, major changes, and complex problems can all be sources of chronic stress and anxiety.

If you feel like this is you, then you have come to the right place. In this book, I will provide you with all of the tools you need to manage stress, regardless of your life situation. This book will go over the basics of stress management, translating the psychological information into an easy, step-by-step guide that you can follow to bring your own stress and anxiety symptoms under control. By the end of this book, you will know exactly what causes your stress, and what steps you need to take to overcome it. The exercises in this book are here to get you started, but all of the strategies are designed to help you manage stress and anxiety in a sustainable way.

My name is Michael Robertson, and I have helped patients overcome their anxiety for years. During the course of my time as a professional, I have helped to transform the lives of hundreds of patients. My experience talking with people from all walks of life, who struggle to stop overthinking things and manage their anxiety, has given me a thorough understanding of how best to help people deal with these problems on a daily basis. Over time, I have developed an understanding of what works and what does not. Based on these observations of real people, I have seen how these strategies have impacted their lives and what strategies seem to work more often than others. But these techniques are not only for my patients' use - I have also taught them to my family, my friends, and I still use many myself. I can tell you from my own lived experience that this book will improve your wellbeing and the wellbeing of all those around you.

Once you read through the stress management techniques in this book, and apply them to your daily life, you will start to see some dramatic changes. You will feel more relaxed in stressful situations, and more confident in the face of things that once scared you. The heaviness in your chest and the anxieties that plague you will cease to bother you. You will be able to think clearly about the situation at hand, and stop overthinking.

Many people have thanked me for the positive impact that my training has had on their lives. These techniques have helped individuals lower their anxiety right away, and has also equipped them with the stress management tools they need to keep their anxiety levels low for the long-term. The continued success of this training program helped inspire me to write this book, and I am now able to present to you the same guide that I have given to so many patients. This book will provide you with a day-to-day program that is simple and easy for anyone to follow. It will also equip you with the knowledge you need to connect and understand the techniques listed. Anxiety and stress management doesn't have to be difficult or complex. In fact, many of the techniques I outline in this book are so simple that they sound ridiculous to many people when I first suggest them. But once you make these techniques a part of your daily life, you will begin to see how effective they truly are.

With my help and expertise, you will come away from this book fully equipped with the skills, techniques, and knowledge that you need to eliminate your stress and anxiety. You will also be able to manage your stress levels going forward, so that they never rise to a debilitating level again. My hope is that you will have all of the support you need to take back control over your own mental wellness, armed with all of the tools you need to change your life for the better.

Old habits die hard. It's a cliché, but it's true - and especially when it comes to our health and wellness. Another true cliché: human brains are like sponges, in that they constantly soak up information and stimuli from the world around us. Over time, bits of information sink deep into our subconscious, where they form our attitudes, beliefs, and habits. The longer these attitudes and habits go unchallenged, the more fixed they become in our minds, and the more difficult they are to change. This is great news if our attitudes and habits are beneficial, but it becomes bad news if we allow attitudes or habits that are harmful to enter our daily routine. However, just because something is difficult to change does not mean that it is impossible to change. The mental patterns that lead to stress and anxiety are psychological habits, ones that must be broken if you want to enjoy the valuable and significant moments of your life. Depending on how severe your anxiety is and how long you've struggled with it, overcoming these mental habits might be more difficult than you expect. But no matter what, the sooner you start applying these stress management techniques to your life, the easier it will be for you to overcome them. And no matter how difficult it might be to apply these techniques, it's possible for everyone, at any level of stress, to successfully conquer their anxiety. The guide that you are about to read has been proven over and over again to successfully help people overcome their stress - in any profession, and in any social situation. Each chapter of this book will provide you with practical, actionable steps that you can take to apply the research and psychological information to your daily life. These action steps will, over time, start to replace your old mental habits and behaviors. The closer you follow the techniques outlined for you in this book, the less you will think about them. Over time, they too will become habits, but ones that are instead setting you up for confidence and success - rather than stress, fear, or anxiety.

Chapter 1: Stressed? Join the Club and Get Started

If you feel stressed, the good news is that you're not alone. Stress is something that almost every individual experiences at one point or another. Chronic fatigue, a short temper, or constant worrying are all common symptoms of extreme stress - experienced by thousands of people from all walks of life. Stress can come from a number of different sources, including your job (or lack thereof), your finances, your personal life, or your schedule. Feeling like you don't have enough time to finish all that you need or want to do is also a common source of anxiety.

In today's world, *stress* and *anxiety* are hardly uncommon words. From bestselling books, to podcasts, to news articles - it seems like everyone on earth is struggling with some kind of stress or an anxiety-related problem. In fairness, our modern world exposes us to far more media than our ancestors ever consumed. But the contemporary concern about stress may not simply be the inevitable result of saturation in more information. In fact, there is quite a bit of research to suggest that stress and anxiety are on the rise for many other reasons. For example, in 1910, it was reasoned that the average housewife spent about 52 hours a week on housework (Elkin, 2013). But in 1970, despite increases in machine efficiency, that figure was exactly the same (Elkin, 2013). Modern technology and infrastructure may have saved time for certain activities, but it also increased the demand for others. The time saved was instead filled with new and different responsibilities, and the workload has been kept essentially the same (Elkin, 2013).

Now, in 2020, we have even less free time than we did in the 1970s, let alone the 1910s. Whether you're a housewife, a doctor, or an artist, modern technology has simply increased professional and personal expectations of how much work you can reasonably achieve in a single day. Not only do we have far more to do now, but we have much less time in which to get it done.

In 2010, a study by the American Psychological Association (APA) found that 44% of Americans surveyed had experienced a significant increase in stress in the past five years (Elkin, 2013). That same APA study also found that 22% of adults believed themselves to be in fair to poor health, and that the stress levels reported by that group were significantly higher than the rest of the population. Just a few years later, a Harris Interactive study found similar results, where 46% of participants reported that they had experienced a significant increase in stress in the past five years (Elkin, 2013). The Harris study also found that a shocking 80% of people surveyed had reported medium or high levels of stress in the workplace, and 60% of people reported experiencing similar stress levels at home.

So why is the world so stressful? Is it simply because we're busier than we were 50 years ago? In part, yes, but those recent studies aren't just seeing an increase in stress over generations. People are reporting significant increases in stress after just five year periods. Part of the answer can also be found in Alan Toffler's text, *Future Shock* (1970), wherein Toffler found that people experience higher levels of stress when they are exposed to a lot of change in a short amount of time. Fifty years later, we can see the truth in his findings. What have the past few decades been but a constant stream of change? Think of how different the world was - even just 10 years ago. It can be exhilarating to live in a state of continuous change, but it can also make you feel out of control of your own life. More than ever, people live with these extreme levels of uncertainty. This chronic uncertainty can make you feel threatened, at worst, and overwhelmed, at best.

One of the biggest challenges in recent years was the 2008 economic crash. In 2010, just two years into the economic recession, an American Psychological Association study found that 76% of participants reported "money" as a significant source of stress in their lives (Elkin, 2013). At a close second, 65% of participants from the same study reported the economy as a significant stressor. Today, as world finances become more closely intertwined, the economies of all nations become increasingly unstable. The financial infrastructure laid down by past generations is unable to cope with new technology, new business practices, and new global trade relationships. The inevitable result of these large-scale changes is that, on an individual level, we have more insecurity about our money. Jobs may be created, changed, or disappear altogether. The regulations that govern credit, student loans, mortgage payments, and taxes will continue to evolve. As individual bills add up, the stress that we can feel around money continues to increase at a rapid pace.

It may seem that having a good, stable job would eliminate some of this financial stress, but a job can add additional stressors of its own. Job security, inconvenient hours, commutes, deadlines, difficult bosses, office politics, and disrespectful clients are just a few of the ways that jobs can add stress to your life. Even otherwise helpful and efficient technology can create workloads that are much heavier than they were 10 years ago - making even a "good" job stressful to perform every single day.

In 2012, a Harris Interactive study found that 41% of participants felt stressed during the workday (Elkin, 2013). In that same study, 58% of participants reported that they did not know how to successfully manage their stress. Today, those numbers have increased. It's now estimated that 62% of Americans experience a significant amount of job-related stress (Elkin, 2013). The economic cost of that stress, in terms of efficiency, medical bills, and loss of talent, is estimated to be around $300 billion nationwide (Elkin, 2013). A reported 25% of Americans have used their paid personal or sick leave just to get a break from the stress they feel at work, and the same number have reported feeling "often" or even "very often" burned out at their jobs (Elkin, 2013, p.12).

However, while money and work are two extremely common sources of stress, they are far from the only places stress can come from. In your journey toward better stress management, the first step is to determine the areas of your life where most of your stress comes from.

What are the Main Causes of Stress?

As mentioned, money and work are the two biggest causes of stress in the United States. In a 2015 survey conducted by the American Psychological Association, 72% of participants experienced high levels of *financial stress* during the past month, and 77% of participants cited finances as a source of extreme anxiety (Scott, 2020). Financial stress is such a pervasive and common source of stress that many people don't even realize how much time and energy they spend worrying about it. You know that finances are a significant stressor for you if you:

- worry or feel anxious about money
- argue with loved ones about money
- feel guilty about spending money
- are afraid to open letters or answer phone calls from banks and other financial institutions

Financial stress is considered so common because it can take years to overcome. If money is one of your major stressors, it is important to start now to manage your stress, as the effects are not just psychological. Long-term financial stress has been linked to a number of physical symptoms as well, including high blood pressure, headaches, stomach troubles, chest pain, insomnia, chronic fatigue, depression, anxiety disorders, skin problems, diabetes, and even arthritis.

After finances, *work trouble* is another significant stressor that plagues Americans today. According to a recent study conducted by the Center for Disease Control and Protection, Americans today spend 8% more time at work than they did 20 years ago, and 13% more Americans work more than one job (Scott, 2020). Of participants in that same study, 40% reported experiencing extreme stress in the workplace, and 26% indicated that they often feel burned out at work.

However, a high volume of work is just one way that jobs can be stressful. Job insecurity can also be an extreme source of stress, as is dissatisfaction with your job or career. Conflicts with your boss or coworkers can also create a great deal of workplace anxiety. Whether you're treated unfairly or nervous about a major deadline, workplace anxiety doesn't always remain in the workplace. You often carry that stress home with you, where it can negatively impact your personal relationships. Workplace stress has also been linked to a number of physical and mental health symptoms, including chronic fatigue, headaches, muscle tension or pain, stomach problems, heart palpitations, anxiety, depression, and mood swings. Workplace stress can even negatively affect your cognitive abilities, which makes it more difficult to concentrate and make decisions.

You know that work is a significant stressor for you if you:

- use sick days even when you're not sick
- routinely underperform at work

- experience problems in your personal life
- have low creativity or motivation
- have low patience or high frustration levels
- find it difficult to become interested in new information or experiences
- socially isolate yourself

At one point or another, *personal relationships* will cause us to feel some level of stress. It's impossible to get along with everyone all the time. But a relationship can turn toxic when it is bad more often than it is good. Whether it's with a family member, a romantic partner, a friend, or a co-worker - a relationship that has gone sour can cause very high levels of stress. Relationship stress can sometimes be difficult to spot, as the individual stressors will be unique to the people involved. However, there are some relationship stressors that are more common than others. If you are feeling stressed by a close relationship, it may be because you or your partner:

- are too busy to evenly share responsibilities
- have other commitments that block your personal time together
- are not able to communicate clearly
- abuse alcohol or drugs
- have considered ending the relationship
- are overly controlling, manipulative, or abusive

Relationship stressors often manifest themselves physically as sleep problems, depression, anxiety, or chronic fatigue. You may start to avoid the other person, or become easily irritated by them. Either way, these stress-responses almost always make the situation worse, and thus increase your stress levels even more. Personal relationships don't always have to be face-to-face either. People that you communicate with primarily through social media can also be a significant source of stress. Bullying and miscommunication is much more likely to happen remotely than it is in person. Social media also causes you to unfavorably compare yourself to others, which creates stress and anxiety in its own right.

Another major source of stress is *parenting* - no matter how good your children are, or how much you love them. Inevitably, parents find themselves faced with incredibly busy schedules that ask them to juggle children, jobs, and household duties. Perhaps the worst symptom of parental stress is that it can cause you to become harsh, negative, or even authoritarian with your children. All of these stress-responses can decrease the quality of your relationship with your child, and therefore increase your levels of stress.

Busy schedules are far from the only source of parental stress. Financial instability, long working hours, single parenting, tension with your partner or co-parent, or raising a child with physical or cognitive disabilities can all be sources of stress. Parents of children with disabilities are at the highest risk for parental stress, and often report much higher levels of stress than parents of children without a diagnosis or a disability (Scott, 2020).

As well, being *over-scheduled* is an increasingly common stressor in our contemporary lives. Too much to do can cause you to become disorganized and unfocused, which leads to small mistakes like lateness or the loss of important items. A number of factors contribute to being over-scheduled, such as working more than one job, which can stretch out the workday and increase your daily responsibilities. Others may find themselves with too much on their plate because they connect saying "no" with a sense of guilt. Disappointing others carries a significant social energy. You know you're overscheduled when you put off basic tasks like eating or exercising because you "don't have time."

Determining Your Stressors

To help you identify the major stressors in your life, take out a piece of paper or open a blank document on your computer. Divide the paper into two sections: *Internal Problems* and *External Problems*. All of life's stressors can be loosely divided into these two categories.

On one side, begin with the heading "*Internal Problems*". This will include all stressors that are related to you as an individual. Physical, psychological, and emotional stressors are all internal stressors because they affect you personally. Beneath this heading, leave space to list the following stressors: *Health*, *Relationships*, *Personal Beliefs*, *Emotions*, *Life Changes*, and *Money*. Put the items that cause you the most stress at the top of your list, and the items that cause you the least stress at the bottom.

Put a star next to *Health* if you are worried about aging, the diagnosis of a new disease, or symptoms and complications from a preexisting illness. These are all common stressors. Health also doesn't have to be about you. If a loved one struggles with an illness or condition, consider where you place Health on your stressor list.

Put a star next to *Relationships* if you have had an argument with your partner, parent, or child in the past month. Conflicts in other relationships can be stressful as well, so consider any outside of those three. But conflict or tension with the people that you live with can be even worse than conflict with people outside the home.

Put a star next to *Personal Beliefs* if you have had an argument about personal, religious, or political beliefs in the past month. Discussing these topics can be positive opportunities for growth - even if those discussions get lively or heated - but if you would categorize the discussion as a fight or an argument, then it was also a situation that caused you stress. If you have these kinds of arguments a lot, then *Personal Beliefs* may be something that causes you a significant amount of social stress.

Put a star next to *Emotions* if you find it difficult to relate to other people, or if you have experienced a traumatic event in the past. Emotional problems can have a number of different sources and can cause distress by themselves. But when our emotional troubles start to negatively affect our relationships, we start to feel a great deal of stress that can be related to feelings of guilt, inadequacy, or depression.

Put a star next to *Life Changes* if you have experienced the death of a loved one, started a new job, or relocated to a new home recently. All major life events bring their own levels of stress, from a child in college to retirement. Only you can determine the significance of these events, and where to place *Life Changes* on your list. Finally, put a star next to *Money* if you carry significant credit card debt, are worried how to pay your rent, or are worried how to provide for your family. Money troubles can take many different forms, but these three stressors are the most common and, unfortunately, difficult to solve. Familiar solutions like a change in workplace or financial support from loved ones is helpful, but difficult to sustain in the long term.

Now take a look at your list. No matter what, you should focus on the top three items you placed on your list, as these three items were deemed significant by you - and this is important. However, all starred items need attention, and if you starred more than four items on your list, then you should consider *internal* stressors as your primary source of stress. If so, this is the area where you need to focus the most energy when it comes to stress management.

Now, move to the second half of the page, and begin with the heading *"External Stressors"*. These are stressors that come from social or professional sources, places that we often have very little control over. Beneath this heading, leave space for three items: *Occupation, Discrimination, Environment*. Write them in order of significance, with the first item being the highest stressor and the last item being the lowest stressor.

Place a star next to *Occupation* if you typically work more than 40 hours a week, or if you've experienced conflict at work in the past month. The American Psychological Association estimates that 60% of Americans experience extreme levels of work-related stress, so if this stressor is number one or two on your list, you're far from alone (Legg, 2016). Job-related stress can come from many sources, but long hours and workplace conflict have been the most closely linked to physical health consequences, and are most likely to negatively impact your personal and professional lives.

Put a star next to *Discrimination* if you have experienced physical, emotional, or social distress because of your race, ethnicity, gender identity, sexual orientation, or any other identity you have. Discrimination can cause extreme amounts of external stress, as it can prevent you from receiving professional opportunities, strain your social relationships with people outside of your identity group, and even put you in physical danger. Discrimination, while felt locally, primarily occurs on a large-scale social level, and has far reaching consequences, including limiting opportunities for the disenfranchised. While unfortunate, the roots of discrimination often lie far beyond what an individual person can change by themselves, and thus exist as an external stressor, rather than an internal stressor. However, this raises an interesting case. In America, being white, being born an American citizen, or living as male can all endow significant social privileges, including some that are not always noticeable. If you fit these categories, then yes, jokes about white people may make you uncomfortable; as may jokes about "Americans". But your reaction to these particular social situations should be considered internal stressors, not external stressors. It might annoy you when someone talks about how terrible men are, but that's not a situation that puts you in danger or disenfranchises you on a broad, social scale - and thus there is no external stress placed upon your experience - it is an inner reaction.

Finally, put a star next to *Environment* if you feel unsafe in the neighborhood where you live or work. Feeling unsafe can cause huge amounts of stress, making it impossible for you to relax when you are in that environment. Safety concerns can come from many different places, including crime, discrimination, or even environmental pollutants.

Now, take a look at your list. The first item you placed on your list should be your largest focus going forward, as that area of your life causes you significant levels of stress. If you starred more than one item on your list, then you should consider External Stressors as a major cause of stress. Looking at both lists, if you starred more than four *Internal Stressors* and more than one *External Stressor*, then you experience high stress levels throughout multiple areas of your life. If that's the case, then it is especially important to focus on your major stressors (top three for *Internal*, top one for *External*). If you learn to successfully manage stress in these areas, you will experience a significant amount of relief, and possibly even make it easier for you to cope with stress in other areas of your life.

Chapter 2: Do You Understand Stress?

You've now successfully determined the main sources of stress in your life. But what exactly *is* stress?

Psychologically speaking, stress has historically been defined in two ways: *stimulus-based* or *response-based*. The stimulus-based definition of stress suggests that stress comes from pressure. The greater the pressure, the more stress you feel. We can all tolerate low levels of stress. Our brains would be pretty poorly designed if we couldn't! But there is a certain point when the pressure becomes too much, and your mind and body start to suffer under the strain. While stimulus-based stress builds primarily from external stressors, it can then also relate to internal stressors - a cumulative nature of stress. In other words, the build-up of many tiny stresses can be just as harmful as one big, traumatic event (Butler, 1993).

The response-based definition of stress, on the other hand, suggests that stress specifically comes from negative stimuli. This approach focuses less on what causes the stress, and instead focuses on the severity of your body's reaction to stressors. This definition explains why something that might be exciting or even trivial to one person may be an extreme source of anxiety for another person. The ways in which the body responds to stress were first divided into three measurable stages by Hans Selye in the 1950s. According to his research, the first sign of stress in the body is what he called an "alarm reaction" (Selye, 1956). Today, we commonly call this the "fight-or-flight" response. Essentially, this is what happens when your brain registers a potential threat. Whether that threat takes the form of an oncoming train, a looming rent payment, or a gory scene in a horror film, your brain and body will respond in the same way. Once a threat is detected, your brain starts to produce different chemicals, and asks all of the systems of the body to be on high-alert so that you have the strength, energy, and alertness you need to deal with the situation. The stress response is, in theory, an amazing survival tool. It transforms us into superbeings, and heightens all of our senses in order to combat danger. But if you are in a constant state of stress, then the stress response never goes away. Your body never has the chance to go back to its normal "rest-and-digest" state, where you can relax.

If you sustain a fight-or-flight reaction long enough, your body goes into the second stage of stress, what Selye calls "resistance" (1956). In this stage, your brain is in conflict with itself. Your conscious mind knows that you are not in immediate danger, but your subconscious mind is not convinced. Unfortunately, it's the subconscious mind that triggers and subdues the stress response. You may be able to convince yourself that everything is fine, but it takes a lot more than willpower to convince your body. This is the stage where you start to treat your stress in order to relieve it. But there are healthy and unhealthy ways to cope with stress. If we are not fully aware of what happens inside our body, we can easily fall into negative coping methods like anger, manipulation, or avoidance. If this resistance stage continues for too long, your body will enter the third stage, what Selye calls "collapse" or "exhaustion" (1956). It is at this point that you start to see physical or mental health problems appear, which are directly related to your stress.

We know now that both definitions of stimulus-based and response-based stress are useful and important. It is very important to know where your stress is coming from, but it is also important to understand why you respond to your stressors the way that you do. Your personality, life circumstances, past traumas, and sometimes your genetics all combine to determine what pressures cause you to feel stress and the methods you naturally reach for to cope with your stressors.

Stress is dependent on two factors: the *demands* being placed on you by the situation, and the *resources* that you have to meet those demands (Butler, 1993). If the situation asks you to do more than you are capable of, then you start to feel stress. The catch, however, is that *demands* and *resources* are not objective words. Unfortunately, stress is not based in reality, stress is based in how you personally perceive the situation. Your thoughts, attitudes, beliefs, and fantasies all combine to create a unique understanding of yourself and your situation. If you believe that you are not able to meet a challenge, or not capable enough to successfully navigate a situation, then you will begin to feel stress. This occurs even if your belief is unfounded or simply untrue. Stress, then, can be seen as a kind of relationship. A relationship between you and the world around you. Stress arises when something in your life, whether it's another person, a bill, or a workload, drains you of all your resources and therefore puts you in danger (Lazarus & Folkman, 1984). The danger of unemployment, divorce, or the inability to provide a good home for your children are all very real situations that can trigger your body's stress responses. It could even be the threat of physical danger, like exhaustion.

Because stress is about how you perceive a situation, and not just the situation itself, there are as many different kinds of stressors as there are humans in the world. What makes you shrivel up inside with dread might seem mundane or boring to someone else. Something that makes you feel excited, or projects that you enjoy working on, might set another's teeth on edge. There's no such thing, then, as a stressor that's "not a big deal." If the situation causes you to feel stress, then it's a big deal to you. It doesn't make you weak or incapable, it's just a part of who you are. The solution is not to "stop" feeling stressed about something, rather, the solution is to figure out what it is about that situation that is causing you to feel stressed. Anxiety and stress mean that something about the situation in front of you feels threatening. For whatever reason, you feel like you don't have the time, energy, intelligence, or finances to handle the task in front of you. That is the feeling that we call "stress," and that is what we need to know within ourselves.

The Study of Stress

Stress is something we talk about so much that often we don't take a step back to think about what it really is. If you had to describe stress, what would you say? What words would you use? How is stress different from anxiety or worry? Sure, these distinctions might seem more important to a psychologist than to us. But the ability to understand exactly what the feeling of stress is, and how it might differ from other feelings, is very important to help us manage our stress appropriately.

While a common word now, the word "stress" first entered the English language in the 1300s. When it was first used, it was simply a shortened alternative to the word "distress," and was used primarily to describe physical hardships like pain, torture, or starvation (Stress Definitions from Stress Researchers, 2013).

Of course, the 1300s were a long time ago, but the meaning of the word stress did not truly change until more recently, in the early 1930s and the beginning of modern psychology. In an attempt to better understand how different states of mind can affect our mental and physical wellbeing, psychologists began using the word "stress" to relate to mental and emotional hardship, not just physical pain. Hans Selye was one of the first to define stress in psychological terms, calling it a "non-specific response of the body" to change, or to the perceived need for change (1954, p.1). In other words, the first psychological definition of stress tells us that stress can indeed take many different forms. It also tells us that stress is a response to change, or when you feel like a change needs to be made, such as a deadline, an unpaid bill, or relationship pressure.

Selye continued to research stress, and eventually developed his three stages of the stress response - fight-or-flight, resistance, and collapse (1956). But later, in 1979, he changed his definition slightly, calling stress instead a "perception" (Stress Definitions from Stress Researchers, 2013). In other words, stress became understood as subjective. Not necessarily related to reality, nor a purely physical sensation, but stress instead begins in our mind first. Selye would continue his research and later clarify further, stating that stress does not necessarily occur with all life changes, but it occurs when we feel we have to make a change and we don't know how to successfully achieve it (Albrecht, 1979). For example, if a major deadline looms, you know that you need to work faster. But you don't know how to work faster without burning yourself out. The result? Stress. Consider also the stress that comes when you plan a wedding - there are so many things to be done that you don't even know where to start!

It was in 1982 that the psychologists Holroyd and Lazarus suggested that stress could also be measured in terms of your "resources" (1982). For example, if a situation demands more time, money, or energy than you have available, you may develop more stress (Stress Definitions from Stress Researchers, 2013). If, on the other hand, you have enough resources to successfully navigate a situation, then you may feel something else, possibly a feeling of confidence or excitement. You may also not even feel anything at all, and catalogue it simply as a mundane task.

But in 1985, another shift occurred in the scientific world. J.E. Skinner suggested that rather than stress as an internal development, it was instead a reaction to negative, external forces (Kunos & Ciriello, 1992). This created our "stimulus-based" definition; to counter the earlier "response-based" definition (Stress Definitions from Stress Researchers, 2013).

We know now that both of these definitions have grains of truth to them, but the final piece of the stress puzzle wasn't found until 1988, when R.S. Eliot expanded upon the Holroyd and Lazarus definition (Stress Definitions from Stress Researchers, 2013). It was Eliot who first suggested that the stress response was not triggered by how many resources you have, but about how many resources you *think* you have. So stress may be triggered by external events, but it develops internally as a response to those events. Two people with the same resources, one who believes they have enough and another not enough, will feel different levels of stress. In short, it's not the situation itself that causes stress, but the way that you respond to it.

But the story of stress doesn't end there. In 1990, Steinberg and Ritzman determined that stress actually took two basic forms: "overload" and "underload" (Stress Definitions from Stress Researchers, 2013). If you feel overloaded with information, whether too many choices, too much to do, or too much input from other people, then you will begin to feel stress. This idea connects well to Selye's original theories from the 1970s. If you feel overloaded, then your stress is not from feeling incapable of succeeding, but rather, from feeling stuck or confused about the appropriate next step.

On the other hand, you can be underloaded if you feel you do not have the resources to cope with the task in front of you, even something as common and familiar as washing the dishes or answering a text. When you look at your own stressors, consider whether you feel overloaded or underloaded. Do you have too much on your plate? Do you feel completely overwhelmed by the situation(s) in front of you? Or are you afraid that you don't have what it takes to successfully handle the situation? Do you feel that you aren't capable enough?

Just a few years later, in 1992, James Humphrey united overload and underload stress under one common title. Humphrey stated that stress was caused by anything that makes it difficult to maintain "equilibrium" (Stress Definitions From Stress Researchers, 2013)). So whatever disrupts your internal feelings of competence and peace, by this definition, can be considered a cause of stress. These are what we now refer to as "stressors." Whether you feel underloaded or overloaded, you have encountered a situation where it is increasingly impossible for you to feel at peace (Stress Definitions from Stress Researchers, 2013). Your stress response has been activated, and you can't seem to make it go away.

What are the Symptoms of Stress?

You now have a better understanding of what stress actually is, at least from a psychological standpoint. But what are the symptoms of stress? How does stress affect our mental and physical wellness?

Contemporary science understands that what Selye called the "collapse" phase of stress is a very real, physical phenomenon. When your brain feels threatened, for any reason, it will first have your nervous system release a number of different hormones, including adrenaline and cortisol. These hormones are called stress hormones; their job is to change your body chemistry so that you can respond to the threat in front of you. When stress hormones are released, your heart pounds faster, your muscles tighten, your blood pressure rises, your breath quickens, and you become more alert. In the short term, these changes greatly increase your strength and stamina. But in the long-term, they can have some serious side-effects.

Stress can negatively affect any system of the body. It's not only a psychological phenomena. Worse, stress can aggravate pre-existing health conditions, making them much worse or causing flare-ups from conditions that were once under control. Sometimes stress can even cause us to develop conditions that we are genetically susceptible to. Conditions that can be triggered or worsened by chronic stress include (Segal et al., 2020):

- depression and anxiety disorders
- pain
- sleep disorders
- autoimmune disorders
- digestive disorders
- skin conditions (eczema)
- heart disease
- weight problems
- reproductive disorders
- thinking and memory problems

Stress can trigger a number of different conditions throughout the mind and body, even if you are not necessarily predisposed. Not everyone experiences all of these symptoms, and they also have much to do with your situation, lifestyle, mindset, and coping mechanisms.

The most common *cognitive symptoms* of stress are memory problems, inability to concentrate, and poor judgement (Segal et al., 2020). Chronic stress makes it nearly impossible for your brain to focus on what's in front of you because you constantly worry about the stressor. And if what's in front of you *is* the stressor, then you can only worry about what might happen if things go wrong. To properly process new information, your brain needs to maintain a certain level of attention. If you're not focused, it becomes difficult for your brain to store new memories. As such, people who are extremely stressed often forget information or misplace important items, like car keys.

Many people who deal with chronic stress often find it difficult to think positively. Anxious or racing thoughts can sometimes develop, as can a state of constant worry. These symptoms are especially common in people who also have depression or anxiety disorders. All of these symptoms can create further problems in your life, not just in the immediate stressful situation. The more problems you have, the more stressed you become, trapping you in a vicious cycle.

The most common *emotional symptoms* of stress are depression, general unhappiness, anxiety, agitation, moodiness, irritability, and anger (Segal et al., 2020). People who would not otherwise consider themselves depressive or unhappy can find their mood dangerously darkened by chronic stress. Sometimes that stress can develop to the point that it becomes a major depressive episode. Another condition that can be brought on by stress is anxiety, even in someone who otherwise would not consider themself an anxious personality. In fact, stress is so often the trigger for people developing anxiety disorders that the two words are increasingly being used interchangeably. In today's world, with stress on the rise, it is hardly surprising that the number of people diagnosed with anxiety disorders also climbs year by year.

Even if you are not diagnosed with a mental health disorder, stress can still cause you extreme emotional distress. Stress can cause you to feel overwhelmed, lonely, and isolated. By themselves, these feelings are terrible to live with. Over time, these feelings can also develop into mental health problems, even after your stress has gone away. Emotions are powerful forces in the brain. If you spend a long time feeling overwhelmed, that emotion becomes deeply rooted in your view of the world - even if the original cause of that feeling is long gone.

The most common *physical symptoms* of stress are aches and pains, diarrhea and constipation, and nausea or dizziness (Segal et al., 2020). It is extremely common for people dealing with chronic stress to visit the doctor's office and complain of inexplicable aches and pains before they ever visit a psychologist. Unfortunately, it is still unclear whether the phantom pains caused by stress have a direct physical cause, or if they are low-level hallucinations. As well, diarrhea or constipation are both as likely to occur because of the pressure chronic stress puts on the digestive tract. Eating well and exercising can help, but no matter how great your habits, stress can still stop your digestive tract from doing its job properly.

The stress response also elevates your heart rate, and for that reason, some people experience chest pains or heart palpitations when they feel stressed. Those chest pains are definitely not phantom pains. Victorian novels are filled with people who die from fright, lovesickness, or shock, and strangely, those novels are not far from the truth. The strain that chronic stress puts on the heart and circulatory system can absolutely lead to heart disease and in extreme cases, can include cardiac arrest. Loss of sex drive can also occur with chronic stress, as can sexual dysfunction. Those whose immune systems are suppressed may find themselves constantly sick, contracting every cold, flu, and virus that comes their way.

The most common *behavioral symptoms* of stress are eating disorders, sleep disorders, and social withdrawal (Segal et al., 2020). A common response is stress eating, where someone eats, or constantly snacks, but not because they're hungry. Rather, they eat because it triggers the release of serotonin in the brain. Serotonin is a chemical that makes us feel good, bringing a stress eater some temporary emotional relief from the stress they feel. However, stress eating can lead to all kinds of health problems, including rapid weight gain, digestive disorders, and heart disease. Stress eaters rarely reach for salads - instead, they're far more likely to reach for "comfort foods" like ice cream, chocolate, mac n' cheese, or a big juicy hamburger - which can release greater serotonin levels.

On the other hand, stress can also cause someone to lose their appetite altogether. They either forget to eat because they're busy with the problem in front of them, or they intentionally stop eating because they just don't feel like it, or have the energy for it. Either of these habits can lead to a number of different health problems, and can make it far more difficult for the body and brain to cope with other stress-related symptoms.

No matter what symptoms you may experience, they are probably extremely unpleasant. And if you have not noticed any of these symptoms yet, it may be only a matter of time before you do. These symptoms are the primary reason why stress is so detrimental to our health and wellbeing, and halting the progress of these symptoms is the main reason it is so important to manage your stress as early as possible.

Chapter 3: Managing Stress - The Basics

Though stress can wreak havoc on your life, a stress management strategy can seem overwhelming in its own right. Almost always, when I first recommend stress management to people, their first response is that they don't have time, they're too busy, it's too much work, or, most commonly of all, that they've already tried stress management and it didn't work.

But none of these things are true. At least, not if you don't want them to be. If you feel like you don't have the time or you're too busy to manage your stress, don't worry. It's okay to go slow, and go at a pace that works best for you. There are no deadlines in stress management. If you only have 10 minutes a day to spare, that's fine. If you only have 10 minutes a week to spare, that's fine too. The only important thing is to stay committed and put yourself on a regular schedule. Don't tell yourself you'll do it "whenever you have time." If you do that, you'll never get around to it, and give up before you've really even started.

Stress management is a skill, and like all skills, it takes time and practice to learn. You can't master it overnight, no matter how hard you try. So you might as well go slow. Overwhelming yourself will actually increase your stress - the opposite of what stress management is supposed to do. For ideal results, 15 minutes a day is the recommended time to devote to a daily stress management technique (Avoiding Roadblocks to Stress Reduction, 2016). This might sound like a long time, but that 15 minutes can happen during a coffee break, a lunch hour, the moment that you get home from work, or during your morning commute.

If you are resistant to taking on a new project or feel like stress management is simply too much work, just remember that there is no one right way to manage your stress. Everyone's stressors are unique, and everyone's idea of relaxation is different. A beach in the Caribbean might sound like heaven to you, but it might sound like hell to someone else. Don't be afraid to drop or modify a stress management technique if it doesn't work for you. But remember, it may take awhile before many of these techniques start to show results. If you begin to dread your designated 15 minutes of daily meditation, try instead to experiment with different kinds of meditation, or even move on to a different technique entirely.

That being said, try to keep your mind open and give new things a try. Some of these stress reduction techniques might feel a little strange or uncomfortable at first. Some may be familiar to you, while others might be completely new. With increasing amounts of stress in the world, different stress management techniques may have gained mainstream attention. This is both a good and a bad thing. For example, you may have heard of breathing exercises before, or even tried a few of them yourself. But the context in which you were introduced to this concept can sometimes affect the way that you think about it. Try to have an open mind, and give these techniques an honest try before you rule them out. You might be surprised at what starts to work for you once you find a way to work it comfortably into your daily routine.

Most methods and techniques require practice before you get them completely right. Approach stress management the same way you would approach learning to ride a bike or drive a car. You won't do it perfectly the first time. Or the second. Or even the third. Though stress management can seem like an intellectual pursuit, it's not enough to only read about it. Anyone can understand how to drive a car from a simple explanation. But to get behind the wheel is a different kind of learning. When you try out a stress management technique, you get behind the wheel, so to speak. So be patient, be open, and eventually you will get into a style and rhythm that is comfortable for you.

It is very important to practice stress management techniques in a quiet place. Don't wait until you're in a stressful situation to apply these tactics. Think about it like learning an instrument. You need to practice every single day, so that when the day of the concert arrives, you already know what to do. Stress management keeps your stress levels low all the time, so that when you are faced with a stressful situation, you're able to keep calm and confident. However, a quiet place can be difficult to find if you lead a hectic and busy life, so you might have to settle for places that are less glamorous. If you have your own office, that's a great place to practice undisturbed. If you have your own bedroom, that's another good option. Wherever you choose, try to find a space that's relatively private, where you won't be disturbed by others.

Don't feel the need to embark on this journey alone! If someone else in your life is also dealing with stress and anxiety, ask if they want to practice with you. Many self-care routines, like weight loss or going to the gym, are far more effective when you have someone else to do it with. Stress management is the same. You won't feel as alone or self-conscious if you have someone else to practice with, and you're far more likely to stay committed if you have a friend to cheer you on.

Above all, don't expect overnight results. The stress you're experiencing took years and years to build, and so it may take just as long to completely overcome. That's not meant to scare or discourage you, however. Stress management doesn't have to be an invasive or difficult process, but no matter what, it will be a slow one. Don't get impatient with yourself, and don't be too quick to give up on something that isn't yielding the results you want. Go slow, go easy, and don't be too hard on yourself.

How to Measure Your Stress

How can you measure a feeling? Fortunately for doctors and psychologists, stress isn't just something you *feel*. It also affects your behaviors and your physical wellness. For doctors, stress levels can be easily tracked by looking at physical markers, including blood, urine, and even saliva tests that measure the levels of stress hormones present in your body (Figueroa-Fankhanel, 2014). But stress can also be measured from a psychological perspective. Some methods, like observation and interviews, are conducted by professionals. But there are a number of easy strategies you can employ to measure your stress levels on your own. The following 3-Step Process is a very simple one that will help you check in on your own stress levels. It will help you be more aware of how stress affects you, and help you keep track of your progress as you begin employing techniques for stress management.

Do a Gut Check

It may seem obvious, but the first step in measuring your stress level is to simply take a step back and ask yourself, "How do I feel?" A gut check is simply giving yourself a second to check in with your body and mind and determine how you're feeling. Remember that stress presents in everyone's body in slightly different ways. If you find yourself feeling stress, take a moment to observe the situation. How would you rate your stress, on a scale from one to ten (one being very low, ten being extremely high)? Think about your physical symptoms. What's happening in your body? Do you feel pain or tension anywhere? Are you experiencing digestive troubles? Are you having trouble performing sexually? Understanding where and how stress is stored in your body will help you to understand just how stressed you are in any given situation. Sometimes we become so used to dealing with stress that we don't even realize how severe our stress is until our body presents with physical symptoms.

Next, observe your mood. Are you feeling depressed? Anxious? Angry? Just as different people's bodies express stress differently, your mind expresses stress in unique ways too. Learning how you emotionally respond to stress is just as important as learning what your physical symptoms are. Some people become extremely depressed when they're under a lot of stress. Other people feel extremely nervous or anxious. The ways that you emotionally respond to stress will give you clues as to what steps are best for you when it comes to managing your stress successfully.

Use a Stress Gauge

The most commonly used psychological tool to measure stress levels is called the Perceived Stress Scale, or PSS. If you're someone who likes specificity and you want a more concrete way to measure your stress, there are a number of PSS tests and tools available for free online from reliable websites. This test will give you a number between 0-40 to determine how severe your stress levels are. The test asks you to think about your life over the course of the past month, and so it's most useful when conducted on a monthly basis.

Make Yourself a Stress Journal

This can be a physical notebook, a document in your computer, or a dedicated desk drawer. Whatever form it takes, your stress journal is going to be your most important tool as you move forward with your stress management journey. Keeping a record of your stress levels will help you to determine if your stress management techniques are working, and will give you valuable information about yourself that you will need to make the necessary adjustments. Keeping notes in your stress journal does not have to be a difficult task. All you need is 5 minutes a day to update your journal and check in with your emotional and physical wellbeing.

Every day, the first thing you should do when you open your stress journal is rate your stress on a scale from 1-10. This is your gut check, your own personal score. How would you rate your feelings of stress today? If you like, on the first day of every month, take an online PSS test. Pay attention to how your score changes over time. If it's going down, what techniques have you been using that are successful? If it's going up, maybe it's time to change the way you're using your chosen techniques or even try some new techniques altogether.

Once you've recorded your daily score, make a list of any negative physical symptoms you've experienced that day, including pain, fatigue, or other health problems. Finally, write down one word that you would use to describe your mood. Naming your feelings is extremely important for your mental health, but if it's not something you're used to doing, it can sometimes be difficult to find the right words. If you're struggling to describe your emotions accurately, you can find a mood chart online that you can use to help you label your feelings every day.

Recording your stress levels, mood, and physical symptoms every day will give you a lot of information to work with. At the end of your first month, you will be able to look back at your journal and see patterns emerging. You might notice that you usually record having a headache when your stress levels are high. You might notice that you feel irritable all the time, but you only experience anxiety when your stress levels are high. You might find that you were feeling extremely depressed until you started meditating, but once you started that technique, you haven't been feeling so down. Taking just five minutes a day to check in with your feelings can be a stress-reducing technique on its own. Having awareness of how you're feeling and what's going on in your body is perhaps the most important thing you can do when it comes to managing your stress. The unique physical and emotional ways that your body responds to stress is called your "stress signature." Like your fingerprints or your handwriting, your stress signature is unique to you. The more you understand how your body responds to stress, the better you will be at successfully managing it.

Managing Your Stress - The Three-Step Method

Now that you've checked in, determined your major life stressors and created your stress journal, you're ready to begin taking some real steps to manage your stress levels. The simplest stress management approach is called the Three-Step Method (Manage Your Stress: A Three-Pronged Approach, 2016). Stress management is really about finding a way to manage three different things: your stressors, your thoughts, and your stress responses. Different techniques target different categories, but the best way to manage your stress is to find a balance between all three. Stress management is about finding out how your stressors, your thoughts, and your responses all work together to produce the stress that you feel every day. Only focusing on one or the other will only help you to solve one part of the problem.

The Three-Step Method for Stress Management:

1. Manage Your Stressors

Often, stress management techniques focus on eliminating or reducing the events, people, or situations that cause you stress in the first place. While this is not always possible, it is still very important to understand where your stress is coming from in the first place. Stressors can be huge life events like divorce or illness, or small inconveniences like a broken shoelace or a crowded subway. The way that you respond to a stressor won't always correspond perfectly to the severity of the stressor itself. If you experience chronic stress, sometimes a small event can trigger a big response.

Earlier in this book, you completed an exercise to determine where the major sources of stress in your life were coming from. Now it's time to go back to those categories. Look at your major stressors and break them down into specific incidents that you can change or modify. For example, if "work" was a major stressor for you, take a moment now to break "work" down into specific examples. What exactly is it about work that stresses you out? Is it your crowded commute? Are you constantly late? Are you generally dissatisfied with your job, company, or department as a career path?

Now that you've made your list, think about how you can turn these "stressors" into "modified stressors." For example, if you have a crowded commute, is it possible to leave the house earlier or later? If you are constantly late for work, determine what makes you late. Do you need to wake up earlier? Do you need to establish better boundaries with the people you live with in the morning? Do you need to arrange for a more reliable mode of transportation?

We are careful to call these "modified stressors" instead of "solutions" because you don't know if they'll work until you try them. Leaving the house 15 minutes earlier than normal might turn your nightmare commute into a dream. But it also might be difficult for you to wake up that early. You might find that your roommate's car blocks you in, or that 15 minutes is not enough time to catch an earlier train. Your solution might solve part of the problem, but it might not completely eliminate your stress. That's okay! Creating a list of modified stressors gives you a better understanding of what you do and don't have control over in your life. It helps you to think creatively about resolving the situations that cause you stress, rather than becoming further and further trapped in feelings of frustration or anxiety. Breaking your stressors down into small, specific situations can also help to make those situations seem more manageable. "Work" is a huge category, with many potential problems and stressors. But "missing deadlines" is a specific problem that can be solved with specific action steps.

2. Manage Your Thoughts

Remember that stress isn't caused by external events. It's caused by how we *perceive* those events. You might find that there are certain stressors that you have very little control over. You can't always avoid being stuck in traffic or an encounter with unpleasant people. But the way that you think about your situation can go a long way to manage your stress. Change the way that you see a stressful situation and sometimes eliminate your stress altogether!

The next time you find yourself in a stressful situation, try to observe your thoughts in the situation. If your thoughts are negative ("Oh my god, what am I going to do? I hate this. I can't believe this is happening..."), then you might need to tackle the way that you think about the stressful situations in your life, especially if they are situations that you can predict. If you hate your long or crowded commute, try to find a way to make it more enjoyable. Make yourself a commute playlist or listen to an audiobook while you sit in traffic. If you have lots of medical appointments, use the time you spend in the waiting room to practice a foreign language or watch an interesting video on YouTube. Whatever the situation may be, try to see what you can gain or learn from it, rather than obsess over how much you hate or dread it. Put all the mental energy that you put into your worry into your enjoyment. At the very least, you can imagine how good you'll feel when the situation is over!

3. Managing Your Responses.

This is where stress management techniques come in. You may not be able to change your stressor, and while positive thinking is always powerful, there are some situations whose silver-linings just aren't bright enough to make a real difference in your stress levels. Techniques like meditation or deep-breathing are techniques that manage the way that your body responds to stress. Meditation won't make your situation disappear, and it may not change your perspective on it. But it will help to reduce the depression or anxiety that you feel in your mind, relieve the physical tension that you feel in your body, and restore your cognitive abilities so that you can continue to work toward solutions. Managing your stress responses often takes the form of lifestyle changes, like exercise or eating healthy. The techniques that you choose can also specifically target your individual responses. For example, if you tend to get headaches when you feel stressed, you might try stretches or breathing exercises that release tension in the neck and shoulders that cause tension headaches. If you experience digestive issues, try to modify your diet to give your gut the extra nutritional support that it needs to keep you happy and healthy in your time of stress.

Chapter 4: Get Rid of Stress and Anxiety

At this point, you've identified your major stressors, you've made your stress journal to record your physical symptoms and emotional responses to those stressors, and now you are ready to apply real techniques. Any and all stress or anxiety-reduction techniques have one ultimate goal - relaxation. This is especially true for techniques that target our thoughts and responses to stressors that we have little control over.

Relaxation is essentially the difference between a successful stress-management technique and an unhealthy coping strategy. Successful stress-management relieves tension in the body and mind, and helps you to face your situation with confidence and a clear head. Coping strategies, on the other hand, cause us to experience even more fear and tension. Avoidance is a big coping strategy that many people employ because it solves the problem in the short-term. But procrastination, ignoring problems, and cancelling commitments, while they remove the stressful situation in the moment, have a way of creating even more stress later on. Other coping strategies like lashing out at others in anger, pulling an "all-nighter" to get projects done on time, or numbing yourself with drugs and alcohol may also seem like confronting the problem, but they too make your situation much worse.

Relaxation is the core of stress management because it both helps you to relieve the negative symptoms of your stress and helps you to approach difficult situations with confidence. Relaxation relieves the tension in your body, while it also heals and prevents the negative physical effects of chronic stress. It also lifts your mood, clears your mind, and shields you from the negative emotional and cognitive effects of stress. Relaxation is how you relieve your negative feelings without an attempt to escape or suppress them. Once you've released the tension from your mind and body, you can then approach your problems with a clear head, instead of merely succumbing to fear responses.

There is nobody who doesn't want to feel relaxed. But the number one obstacle to a successful incorporation of relaxation techniques is time management. Often, people feel stressed because their lives are busy. If you have too much on your plate, then relaxation techniques can seem like just one more item to add to your list, one that you may not be able to prioritize over other items that you feel are more important.

However, relaxation techniques do not have to be an invasive part of your day. If you feel like you have too much to do, then a second look at your schedule could be a simple technique to manage your stressors all by itself. But the most important thing to remember is that relaxation is... well, important. Really important. Relaxation techniques incorporated into your daily routine will improve your ability to perform every single task on your To-Do List. It will also improve your mood, the quality of your relationships, and your general feelings of happiness and wellbeing. Through the relief of physical tension, relaxation techniques are also beneficial, and perhaps even necessary, for your physical health. If you can find the time to brush your teeth or take a shower every day, then you can definitely find the time to focus on relaxation.

To successfully use these techniques, the first thing to do is set aside a specific time every day for relaxation. It doesn't matter if it's in the morning or at night. It doesn't matter if you'll be at home, at work, or even in your car. The idea is to choose one specific time for relaxation so that nothing else can take precedence over it. If 10:45-11am is your set relaxation time, then nothing else should be scheduled during that time - no meetings, no phone calls, no hanging with friends. Keep this in mind when you set your relaxation time. It's best to choose a time when you can be by yourself in a quiet space and control any unexpected interruptions. For this reason, most people find that the first 10-15 minutes after they wake up or right before they go to bed are the best times for relaxation, but only you can know which time is best for you.

I have suggested 15 minute blocks, but if that seems like too much, you can set aside as little as 5 minutes a day for relaxation. Many techniques are simple, and require no preparation or props. Some people prefer to set themselves several 5 minute relaxation blocks throughout the day. Others would rather give themselves 15-20 minutes every day. Again, there's no right or wrong answer, as long as you're consistent and committed. No matter how long it is, when your relaxation time comes, put everything aside and focus on your chosen technique. That being said, your relaxation period should be practiced daily. Unfortunately, your body doesn't store relaxation. So a daily relaxation practice of 5 minutes will be much more effective than if you employ a relaxation technique once a week for a full hour (Davis et al., 2008).

If you struggle to find an appropriate time to relax, ask yourself two questions: When do I need to relax the most? And when can I break away from external demands to take some time for myself? If you find it's a struggle to get ready or motivated in the morning, then you might want to practice relaxation right after you wake up, or even in the car on your morning commute. Many people find that relaxation in the morning helps them to face the day with confidence, and even helps motivate them to get moving in the morning when they would normally be sluggish.

However, other people have found that relaxation in the middle of the day provides a welcome break from the stress of their busy schedule. Take a quiet moment during a lunch break or simply close your office door for 10 minutes so that you can remain undisturbed. This will help you relieve whatever stress has built up during the day. It can also help you to handle stressful situations faster, and return to your day feeling calm and refreshed. A popular time for many people is just before they leave for work, or right after they come home, especially if work is a major source of stress for you. Relaxation just before you go to bed is another popular time, especially for people who experience sleep problems as a physical symptom of stress.

Relaxation: The Basics

Relaxation is the opposite of stress. Relaxation techniques allow your body to come out of its flight-or-flight response, soothing and even eliminating the symptoms of stress. Relaxation techniques have been proven to slow your heart rate and lower your blood pressure. They slow your breathing rate, improve your digestion, and can even help you to maintain healthy blood sugar levels. No matter what your stress symptoms are, relaxation can help to relieve it. Relaxation brings your body from fight-or-flight into a state called rest-and-digest. Your body stops the production of stress hormones and increases blood flow to the muscles, which in turn relieves pain or tension in those areas.

But relaxation doesn't just relieve the physical symptoms of stress. It improves your concentration, mood, and sleep quality. Daily relaxation practices have been linked to higher energy levels, lower levels of anger and frustration, and greater confidence and self-esteem. And the best part is that all relaxation techniques work equally well. You don't need to choose a specific relaxation technique to help your digestion, nor one to lift your mood, nor one to lower your heart rate. Relaxation techniques are holistic, which means that they heal the entire body all at once. Whatever symptoms you experience, you only need to choose one technique to heal *all* the symptoms of stress present in your body.

There are a few different kinds of relaxation techniques to choose from. If you're like most people, you'll find that some techniques work better for you than others. That's okay! No technique is "better" or "worse" than any other. It simply depends on your unique body, attitude, and stress signature.

Autogenic Relaxation

Autogenic is a word with Greek roots, and means "something that comes from within" (Mayo Clinic Staff, 2020, "Relaxation…"). Autogenic relaxation techniques use visual imagery and awareness of the physical body to reduce your stress. Often, these techniques ask you to repeat a certain word or phrase in your mind that helps you to relax, especially in your muscles. A common example is to imagine yourself in a peaceful setting, and then focus on controlled, relaxed breathing in order to slow your heart rate. Some autogenic techniques ask you to focus on specific parts of the body and relax your muscles one by one.

Progressive Muscle Relaxation

This technique asks you to tense and then relax individual muscles, one-by-one, until the whole body is relaxed (Mayo Clinic Staff, 2020, "Relaxation..."). This technique is especially good for those who experience muscle tension or pain as a physical symptom of stress, but it's worth it for anyone to try, regardless of their stress signature. After they try this technique, many people find that they *do* in fact experience tension in their muscles, but they were so used to that tension that they didn't even realize it! This technique helps you to become more aware of physical sensations in the body. It provides a greater understanding of how your body carries stress and which parts of your body are particularly sensitive to stress. Often these techniques will ask you to start with your toes and work your way up, or start at the top of your head and work your way down. Typically, you tense your muscles for five seconds, and then release them for thirty.

Visualization

This technique asks you to imagine a peaceful place or situation to help you feel safe and relaxed, no matter where you are in real life (Mayo Clinic Staff, 2020, "Relaxation..."). Visualization techniques incorporate all of your senses; imagine smells, sights, sounds, and feelings that are pleasant and comforting to you. For example, if the ocean is a place where you feel peaceful and relaxed, don't just imagine what the sea looks like. Try to hear the sound of the waves, smell the salt water, and feel the warm sun on your skin. Visualization techniques are most easily done with your eyes closed in a quiet spot. It's often recommended that you wear loose or comfortable clothing when you visualize. Many visualization techniques will also ask you to focus on your breathing.

More Advanced Relaxation Techniques

The previous three techniques are the most basic and universally accessible, but they are far from the only relaxation techniques available to you. Again, no technique is "better" or "worse" than any other. Just because a technique is more advanced doesn't mean it will work better. Don't overlook any technique until you've given it a try. You may find that a simple technique is the most effective for a complex problem. That being said, if those three techniques don't work for you (or if you simply want to expand your relaxation practice), there are many other techniques that have been successfully employed by people all over the world, from all walks of life.

Deep breathing is a technique that simply asks you to focus on your breathing. Breathing exercises often ask you to take deep, long breaths. Different breathing exercises can be more or less complex, but if you simply take five minutes a day to focus on breathing slowly and deeply, it can yield some amazing results.

Massage is often the first thing people think of when they think of relaxation, and there is a reason for it. Massages help to relieve stress-related tension in the body. Sometimes, chronic stress has caused our muscles to become so tense that they can't relax without external help. Massage therapists use a number of different techniques to help chronically tensed muscles to relax. In some cases, chronic muscle tension can even cause your bones to move out of place. Many massage therapists also help correct this, and ease your bones back into their natural place.

Meditation is another practice that has become more and more popular. Though it can take a variety of forms, meditation encourages you to focus your mind 100% on the present moment. Meditation can feel like a challenge, especially if you have a mind that likes to whirl and leap from thought to thought. But its benefits have been touted by people as varied as religious leaders, CEOs, psychologists, and artists around the world.

Tai Chi is a relaxation technique that has its roots in ancient Chinese medicine. Tai Chi involves slow, practiced movements, performed in a certain sequence, that help to release tension in both mind and body. Many people around the world feel comfortable with their own personal tai chi routines, but as a beginner, there are many videos online that you can follow to learn the movements.

Yoga is another relaxation technique that focuses on the flow of specific movements in order to relieve stress and tension. Yoga has its origins in India, but is currently practiced by millions of people all over the world. The movements of yoga are often more intense than those of tai chi, and sometimes involve deep stretches or complicated poses. However, there are many different kinds of yoga, and none of them need to be advanced. You can sign up for a class at a local yoga studio, or you can buy your own yoga mat and follow any of the thousands of instructional videos available for free online.

Biofeedback is a technique that has also become more and more popular as modern technology enables us to better understand how stress affects our brain waves. Biofeedback monitors your brain activity, and helps you to identify patterns of stress, relaxation, anxiety, and even mood states like depression or anger. This might sound complicated, but biofeedback monitors are increasingly available for purchase online, and at cheaper prices than you might think. The idea behind biofeedback is that, if you can learn to recognize stressed and relaxed brain states, then you can make much better adjustments to your lifestyle in order to promote relaxation and reduce stress.

Tips for Success

There are so many relaxation techniques out there, it can be hard to know where to begin or which ones might be the best for you. It is important to always be patient with yourself, and give something a fair try before you decide that it doesn't work for you. That being said, here are some tips that you can keep in mind to ensure success and make your chosen techniques more beneficial.

No matter which relaxation techniques you choose, it is advisable to do it in a cool and quiet space where you will not be disturbed (NHS Inform, 2020). While you certainly want to be comfortable, stress can increase your heart rate and actually cause your body temperature to rise slightly. Make sure that your relaxation space is cool to help lower your body temperature and make it easier for your body to calm itself down.

It is also advisable to lie down or sit on the floor with your legs crossed. Unless you've chosen a technique like yoga or tai chi that requires movement, it is rarely comfortable to relax while you stand or sit upright. Lying down is, of course, the most comfortable position of all, but many people find it beneficial to sit cross-legged because that's not something they normally do. Sitting on the floor can also become part of your relaxation routine, as it signals to the brain that it is time to calm down.

If you can, take off your shoes and try to wear comfortable clothing. Tightness and discomfort will make it that much more difficult for your body to relax. The more comfortable you are, the easier it will be for your body to release any pent-up tension. And the more pleasant you can make your relaxation time, the more likely you are to stick with it!

If you can, try to close your eyes (NHS Inform, 2020). This may intimidate you or even seem silly, but with your eyes closed you are free from any potential distractions in your environment. Even if your exercise is just breathing, close your eyes to help you focus purely on relaxation, and decrease the likelihood that your mind will start to wander. Increased focus can also speed up the relaxation process, and allow your body to settle into the technique more quickly.

Finally, regardless of what technique you chose, always try to focus on your breathing. Deep, slow breathing automatically calms your nervous system and floods your bloodstream with oxygen. It is very difficult to maintain stress and tension when your breathing is slow and deep. This is the reason that slow, deep breathing works as a relaxation technique all by itself, and is a critical element of any successful relaxation technique.

Depending on when and where you chose to practice relaxation, you may not be able to follow all of this advice to the letter. For example, it's impossible to close your eyes or sit on the floor if you've decided to relax during your morning commute. But if you don't see the results you want with your chosen technique, you may want to consider a change in your time, place, or method so that you can better incorporate some of these strategies. While these tips are helpful for any relaxation technique, there are some strategies you can try that are unique to specific strategies.

Success Tips for Deep Breathing

Anxiety can sometimes dramatically disrupt your ability to breathe, and cause you to feel faint, dizzy, or nauseous. If you choose a breath-based technique, or need assistance to regulate your breath during any chosen technique, there are a few things you can do to help yourself take even, regular breaths.

One easy way to check in with your breathing is to place one hand lightly on your chest, and the other on your stomach. You want your stomach to move slightly more than your chest when you breathe. When you place your hands on your body, it helps your mind to focus on that area, and makes it easier to pay close attention to your breathing patterns. With your hands on your body, you will also feel your heartbeat slow down, which lets you know that your focused breathing is working (Puddicombe, 2011).

If at all possible, try breathing in through your nose and out through your mouth. This kind of breathing helps to circulate air throughout your respiratory system, and helps to cool your brain and stimulate the major nerves in the throat. When your mind is focused on your breathing, it eliminates distractions and pulls your mind from its spiral into anxiety-inducing thought patterns.

Success Tips for Visualization

If you choose visualization as your preferred technique, or if you would like to incorporate visualization into another technique, you may find that it's sometimes difficult to focus on the suggested image. There is no right or wrong image to visualize, but no matter what, you want to create a mental picture of a space where you feel safe. This place can be real or imaginary, as long as it's a space where you feel rested and calm. This might sound obvious, but it's important to keep this in mind if you start to try visualizations or guided meditations. For example, if the ocean is an environment that stresses you out in real life, a guided meditation that asks you to imagine the coast or beyond is probably not a good choice for you.

Remember that visualization is most effective when it engages all of the senses (Puddicombe, 2011). If you struggle to maintain your visualization, try to move through your senses one at a time. Ask yourself, what does my comfortable place look like? What can I see? What can I hear, smell, or feel? The more sensory detail you can imagine, the more real your relaxation space will feel, and the more relaxed you'll feel.

Chapter 5: Relaxation Tips

As more and more people experience high levels of stress and anxiety, more and more people are also invested in sharing techniques for relaxation. Once you choose the technique you want to try, it's extremely easy to find the guidance you need online to do it entirely by yourself. However, the wealth of information out there can be overwhelming for some people, and sometimes it's hard to know which sources are reliable. For this reason, I've compiled some easy exercises and a variety of techniques to help get you started. I would recommend that you try all of these techniques at least once to better understand what works best for you. Once you become more comfortable with a specific technique, you will feel more confident to branch out and perform your own research.

Breathing Techniques

Exercise #1 - Simple Belly Breathing

Sit in a comfortable position on the floor with your back straight and your legs crossed. Place one hand lightly on your chest and the other over your stomach.

Breathe in deeply through your nose. Feel your hands move as your body expands with air. The hand on your stomach should move slightly more than the hand on your chest.

Exhale through your mouth, releasing as much air as you possibly can. Contract your stomach muscles slightly to push out as much air from your lungs as possible. As you exhale, the hand on your stomach should move inward toward your body, while the hand on your chest should move very little.

Continue to breathe in deeply through your nose and out through your mouth for the duration of your relaxation time. Pay attention to the movements of your hands as they rise and fall with each breath. Mentally count to ten each time you exhale.

If you find it difficult or uncomfortable to sit up, you can do this same exercise while comfortably on your back. If you would rather lie down, you can choose to put a small healing stone or crystal on your stomach instead of resting your hand there.

As you breathe deeply from your belly, you stimulate the vagus nerve, the longest nerve in the body. Stimulation of the vagus nerve helps your body to lower your heart rate, and in the long term, helps to lower your blood pressure.

Exercise #2 - Deep Breathing with Affirmations

Find a quiet place to sit comfortably and close your eyes.

Breathe in deeply through your nose, and exhale through your mouth. Repeat this three times. When you take your fourth breath in, imagine that the air you're breathing is filled with peace and calm. You can even imagine breathing in a relaxing color, bits of stardust, or any other image that you associate with positivity and tranquility.

When you next exhale, imagine that you're breathing out all of the stress and tension stored up in your body. You can even imagine that your exhale is a noxious color or thick like mud. Whatever you imagine negativity to look like, imagine it leaving your body.

On your next, fifth inhale, think of a word or phrase that fills you with peace, calm, and confidence. It can be something as simple as "I breathe in peace and calm," or as specific as "I'm allowed to change my mind about people," or even something empowering like "I can do this!" When you exhale, repeat your affirmation to yourself. Continue to repeat your affirmation with each inhale and exhale for the duration of your relaxation time.

Body Scans

Exercise #1 - Body Scan Meditation

Lying down is the best position to perform a body scan, but if that's not comfortable or possible for you, then this meditation can also be easily completed while you sit up in a comfortable position.

Take a deep breath through your nose, and exhale through your mouth. If you find your shoulders rising and falling dramatically with each breath, try to focus on breathing from your belly rather than your chest. Take three deep, belly breaths.

Continue to breathe slowly and deeply, but now shift your attention to your feet. Observe any sensations you feel in your feet. No matter what you feel, whether it's pain, tension, comfort, heat or cold, try to simply observe and accept it. Take note of any sudden emotions that come up in response to the feelings in your feet.

If you notice any feelings that are uncomfortable, focus on them now. Continue to breathe slowly and deeply. With each exhale, imagine all the pain, tension, or discomfort that you feel leaving your feet and evaporating into the air.

When you're ready, slowly move up your body, and repeat this practice of awareness until you have gone all the way up to the top of your head. Spend two or three breaths becoming aware of each part of your body, but spend extra time anywhere that you experience pain, tension, or discomfort. After you've finished the meditation at the top of your head, record in your stress journal anywhere that you noticed pain or tension in your body. The next time you perform this relaxation technique, check if you experience discomfort in the same areas.

Exercise #2 - Quick Top Down Body Scan

Lay or sit comfortably in a quiet place.

Close your eyes. Breathe in deeply through your nose, and exhale through your mouth. Repeat this three times.

Now bring your awareness to the top of your head. Notice any sensations that you experience there. Remain aware for three full breaths, and simply notice how you feel. If you experience any pain, tension, or discomfort, stay there for three more breaths. With each exhale, imagine the pain or tension leaving your body to evaporate into the air.

Now move your awareness down your body, and spend at least three full breaths on each area of the body. Spend three extra breaths anywhere in your body where you experience discomfort, and visualize the tension leaving your body. Once you have finished the meditation with your feet, record any areas where you felt pain or tension in your stress journal. If you finished the meditation before the end of your relaxation time, return to each of the parts of your body that experienced pain or tension. Lay your hands gently over the afflicted part of the body. Visualize warm, healing energy entering your body. Visualize the pain evaporating into the air like steam rising off the surface of warm water. Extend this visualization for the duration of your relaxation time.

Progressive Relaxation and Physical Meditation

Progressive Relaxation

Progressive relaxation is a technique that asks you to briefly tense and then relax individual muscles in the body. For these exercises, you will focus on different muscle groups, and move progressively from one to the next until you've relaxed all parts of the body. You can simply memorize the order of the muscle groups, or you can use an audio recording or cue cards to help prompt you to move from one group to the next.

Exercise #1 - Muscle Group Progressive Relaxation

To begin, lay down on the floor or on a comfortable bed. Take a deep breath in through your nose, and exhale through the mouth.

On your second inhale, tense the first muscle group, and keep the muscles tensed for 4-10 second, but not to the point of pain. When you exhale, suddenly and completely release the muscles. Don't try to gradually relax them. Unclench completely as soon as you breathe out, and enjoy the relief as tension leaves your body. Simply breathe slowly and deeply for 10 to 20 seconds before you move on to the next muscle group. You will experience some feelings of relief every time you relax, but make a mental note of any muscle groups that feel especially good. These are places where you carried tension before you began the exercise.

Continue until you have tensed and released all muscles groups.

The Muscle Groups, and How to Tense Them (Freeman, 2009):

- Hands: Clench them
- Wrists and Forearms: Extend up from the body, and bend the hands back at the wrists.

- Biceps and Upper Arms: Clench the hands into fists, bend the arms at the elbows, and flex the biceps.
- Shoulders: Raise them up toward the ears.
- Forehead: Wrinkle into a deep frown.
- Eyes and Nose: Clench the eyes shut as tightly as you can (if you wear contact lenses, you should remove them while performing this exercise).
- Cheeks and Jaw: Smile as widely as you can.
- Mouth: Press your lips together as tightly as you can. Be aware of any tension that accumulates elsewhere in the face.
- Back of the Neck: Press the back of your head against the floor or pillow.
- Front of the Neck: Touch your chin to your chest.
- Chest: Inhale deeply through the nose, and hold your breath for 4-10 seconds.
- Back: Arch your back up away from the floor or bed.

- Stomach: Suck in the muscles as tightly as you can. Be aware of any tension that appears in the chest or lower back.
- Hips: Press the buttocks together as tightly as you can.
- Thighs: Clench the muscles as tightly as you can.
- Lower Legs: Point the toes back toward your face. Then point your toes downward, and arch your feet. Be aware of any tension that appears in the thighs or hips.

Exercise #2 - Top Down Progressive Relaxation

Find a quiet and comfortable place to lay down. Inhale deeply through the nose, and exhale through the mouth. Repeat this three times.

Now bring your awareness to your forehead and the top of your head. Notice any tension in the muscles there as you breathe in. On the exhale, intentionally and suddenly release that tension. If you don't feel some relief, repeat this procedure one more time.

Now move progressively down the body, and bring your awareness to the muscles in each part of your body. Anywhere that you experience tension, intentionally and suddenly release it on your exhale. Take an extra breath in areas that experience extreme amounts of tension.

Once you've finished the exercise at your feet, record in your stress journal any areas that you felt were particularly tense. The next time you repeat this technique, compare your notes. Were the same areas carrying tension?

Physical Meditation
Tai Chi - The Basics

Tai Chi is a form of physical meditation that comes from an ancient Chinese spiritual practice called Qi (or Chi) Gong. The "chi" in both of these words comes from a Mandarin Chinese word that loosely translates into English as "spirit" or "energy." In traditional Chinese medicine, your chi is your body's life force, the vital energy that flows throughout your body, healing and restoring your organs and muscles. According to Qi Gong, if chi becomes sluggish or clogged in its journey through the body, then you become sick, both physically and mentally. All Qi Gong meditations are focused on moving chi more fluidly throughout the body.

This might sound like a bunch of hocus pocus, but modern medicine is discovering greater links that connect the concept of chi with a sound scientific basis. We now understand that all parts of the body are interconnected, and that pain or tension in one part of the body can lead to negative physical symptoms throughout multiple organ systems. We also know that our psychology is intimately tied to our physical bodies. Mood states like depression, anxiety, and stress can express themselves as physical symptoms of illness.

Tai Chi is essentially a sequence of practiced, fluid motions that are designed to move chi throughout the body. A focus on the slow, measured poses of tai chi takes your mind off of your stress and brings awareness to your physical body. Daily tai chi practice has been increasingly linked to a number of different physical and mental health benefits, a major one of which is stress reduction. As tai chi becomes more popular in the west, it has become easier and easier to find tai chi classes in local yoga studios, meditation centers, and gyms. There are also a number of tai chi instructional videos online that you can follow for free in the comfort of your own home.

Yoga - The Basics

Perhaps the form of physical meditation most commonly practiced around the world is yoga. Though many people see yoga as a kind of exercise, this practice originated in India as a form of meditation, and knowledgeable yoga instructors will bring a spiritual element into their classes, no matter how much of a sweat you work up.

Yoga can appear quite intimidating to beginners, but it does not have to be difficult or strenuous. A simple yoga flow will take you through a series of stretches, and the instructor will often guide your thoughts toward positive images or phrases to think about as you move through the flow. An extremely popular practice around the world, most cities and towns have a local yoga studio where you can take a variety of classes with licensed instructors, and maybe even meet some like-minded people. There are also thousands of free videos that you can follow online in the comfort of your own home. All you need is a yoga mat, some comfortable clothes, and a full water bottle.

Visualization Techniques

Exercise #1 - Simple Visualization for Building a Safe Space

Find a quiet space where you won't be disturbed and take any posture in which you feel comfortable and relaxed.

Breathe deeply in through your nose, and exhale through your mouth. Repeat this three times.

On your fourth inhale, close your eyes. Imagine yourself in a beautiful location, where everything is perfect, peaceful, and utterly relaxed. There is no right or wrong place to imagine, as long as it's somewhere that brings you total comfort and relaxation. You can imagine yourself on a beach, a mountain, in the middle of a forest, or even inside a building.

Imagine yourself calm and relaxed in that space. You can imagine yourself smiling, laughing, sleeping, or doing anything else that you would do if you were completely at peace.

Focus on the sensory details of your space. What do you see? What do you hear, smell, or feel? If you're a food lover imagining yourself eating a delicious meal, what are you eating? What does it taste like? All of the sensory details in your space should be aesthetically and physically pleasing. Spend time with each of the different senses, and fully imagine the details of your safe space.

Remain within this space for the duration of your relaxation time.

Exercise #2 - Inner Beach Visualization

One of my favorite places to be is on the beach, and it appears that I'm not alone. Many people have found that visualizing themselves next to the ocean is a scene that fills them with peace and tranquility.

To visualize your inner beach, find a quiet place where you won't be disturbed. Take any posture that feels comfortable and relaxed.

Close your eyes. Inhale deeply through your nose, and exhale through your mouth. Repeat this three times.

On your fourth inhale, imagine yourself on a beautiful beach. Look out at the sand. What color is it? Take a handful and run it through your hands. Is the sand rocky or smooth? Are there seashells or seaweed along the coast, or is your beach miles of pure, well-kept sand?

Now look out at the water. What color is it? Is it clear turquoise? Dark blue? Gentle green? Steely grey? Look up at the sky and make the same observation. Is the sky purely blue and cloudless? Is there a bright sun or is it a starry night sky? Is there a gorgeous sunrise or sunset on the horizon? Is it overcast? Perhaps you love the romance of rain or weather over the ocean? Now imagine the sound as the waves hit the sand. Time your inhales and exhales to match the rhythm of your inner ocean waves. Remain comfortably on your inner beach for the duration of your relaxation time.

Chapter 6: Calming Your Mind

Anxiety is a psychological condition that can arise from many different sources. For many people, anxiety and its spectrum of disorders develop as a response to stressful or traumatic experiences. But anxiety also has a genetic component. Some people are genetically predisposed to be more likely to develop anxiety disorders than others. Anxiety can also be passed from a mother to a fetus during pregnancy, regardless of genetics. If a mother experiences extreme stress or anxiety during pregnancy, the stress hormones in her body can affect the way that her baby's brain develops (Haas, 2017).

Whether it comes from your environment or your genetics, anxiety is something that deeply affects the way that your brain works. Anxiety can actually restructure your brain, to the point where anxiety disorders are visible on brain scans. However, studies done at Harvard Medical School have also proven that certain relaxation techniques can similarly restructure your brain, much like the "rewiring" effect of anxiety. Using a number of different research methods, the Harvard studies have demonstrated that relaxation techniques, when practiced daily, change the way that your brain processes information, and can transform anxious neural pathways into calm ones (Haas, 2017).

When anxiety becomes "wired" into your brain, it means certain neural pathways develop in your brain in response to stressful situations. Over time, your automatic response to certain stressors is to experience fear, anger, and distress. Your brain immediately goes into fight-or-flight mode when faced with certain stress triggers, even if the situation at hand is not actually dangerous or threatening. So when it comes to your brain, your strongest defense against anxiety is to develop what Harvard researchers call a "relaxation response." This can be achieved when you develop a daily relaxation routine. Just as anxiety causes your brain to enter fight-or-flight when faced with certain stressors, a daily relaxation practice trains your brain to return to rest-and-digest. So, for example, if you take ten minutes every morning to practice deep breathing while you listen to calm music, your brain will learn to relax when you start the practice. Slowly but surely, your brain will begin to anticipate relaxation time. As your designated relaxation time approaches, your heart rate will automatically start to slow, your blood pressure will decrease, and your body will start to come out of its high-stress state. Regardless of the relaxation technique that you choose for your designated practice time, it is always beneficial to practice deep breathing any time you begin to feel anxious. Anxiety disrupts your natural breathing patterns, and causes you to breathe more quickly and shallowly. In the short term, this is intended to help your body conserve its energy to fight off danger. But in the long term, this can cause your brain to become under-oxygenated, and inhibit your ability to think clearly or regulate your emotions. So if you recognize that you feel anxious, take a second or two to breathe in deeply through your nose and out through your mouth. Even just a few rounds of slow, deep breathing can train your brain to stop the release of stress hormones in the body.

However, sometimes it can be hard to recognize when you're anxious. Fears and worries have a way of gnawing at us, occupying our subconscious minds even when we try our best to think about anything else. If you're a chronic worrier, you may want to consider scheduling a "worry time". Just as you schedule yourself a relaxation time, schedule yourself five to ten minutes everyday to think about your worries. This may sound like strange advice, but if you try to bury or ignore your fears, it rarely makes them go away. Instead of letting those fears take over your life, give yourself ten minutes a day to obsess, plan, imagine the worst case scenario, cry, rant, or do whatever else you need to do. For this moment, give into your worries and fully experience your fears. Then, when your ten minutes are up, dry your eyes, clear your throat, and get on with your day. If you find that you start to worry outside of your designated time, stop yourself. Tell yourself to think about it during tomorrow's "worry time".

An alternative strategy is to schedule time to write down your worries and fears in your stress journal every day. When you write, you force your brain to slow down, which stops you from a spiral into pits of anxiety and nervousness. It can also be cathartic to take the time and write down your fears. As your thoughts leave your mind, and fall onto paper, it serves a similar function as venting to a trusted friend. The difference, however, is that the act of writing is private. Sometimes it can be difficult to relax and fully release your thoughts when someone else is present, no matter how strong your relationship with that person may be. If you take the time to slow things down, you are provided with a safe, and completely private way to open up and unleash the thoughts that truly eat away at you. When done just before bed, this technique has been proven to be especially helpful for people who suffer from anxiety and stress-related insomnia (Haas, 2017).

How to Cultivate a Calm State of Mind

A daily relaxation technique greatly contributes to improvement in your emotional and psychological stress symptoms. However, it's also useful to employ simple tactics throughout the day to keep yourself in a calm state of mind. You want your brain to be your friend. You don't want your ability to think to be regulated by your anxiety.

Breathing is something that we humans take for granted, but it can't be stated enough how powerful and valuable breathing is for your body and mind. Slow, deep breathing activates your parasympathetic nervous system. This is the part of your nervous system that regulates unconscious processes in your body. The parasynthetic nervous system controls automatic functions like your heartbeat, digestion, and hormone production. When this part of the nervous system is engaged, your body naturally moves into rest-and-digest mode. When relaxed, your body will typically enter this state. However, rest-and-digest mode is far more important than it sounds. Only in this state can your body heal itself from physical and emotional harm. If your body is in stress mode instead (fight-or-flight) - it cannot fight off diseases, repair wear-and-tear on your body, or filter out toxins. In stress mode, all of these processes are suspended. These processes can only be accomplished when your body is relaxed and your brain feels calm.

Just a few deep breaths when you start to feel anxious or worried can stop your brain from entering fight-or-flight mode. The psychological and emotional power of deep breathing has been most dramatically demonstrated in its effectiveness for military veterans. The trauma and post-traumatic stress that combat veterans experience is so severe that 50% of veterans do not see significant improvement with therapy or medications (Seppala, 2019). However, many studies have found that after just one week of daily deep breathing exercises, veterans suffering from PTSD, including those who were unable to improve their condition through other methods, showed noticeable improvement in their mental wellbeing (Seppala, 2019).

Another recent study found that your breathing patterns change depending on the emotions that you experience. The study recorded the specific breathing patterns common in people who experience anger, fear, happiness, relaxation, and other emotions. Researchers then taught these breathing patterns to a new group of people, who were not given the context of the breathing exercises. When researchers asked the new subject group how they felt after they completed a few minutes of their designated exercise, the participants' emotional responses corresponded almost exactly to their breathing patterns (Seppala, 2019). Many participants who had been taught the "angry" breathing pattern reported feelings of anger or frustration after breathing that way for a few minutes, even though none of them knew that the breathing pattern they had been taught was related to feelings of anger (Seppala, 2019). In essence, the test subjects were able to evoke certain emotions through a change in their breathing patterns. So, taken another way, a focus on slow, deep breathing can also have a direct effect on your mood. Breathing in a "relaxed" pattern tricks your brain into actual feelings of relaxation! Breathing in through the nose and out through the mouth is encouraged in most deep breathing exercises because it stimulates the vagus nerve, part of the parasympathetic nervous system. As mentioned in the belly breathing exercise from Chapter 5, the vagus nerve is one of the longest nerves in your body - and a significant portion of this nerve is connected to the muscles in your throat. So, the act of breathing in through your nose and out through your mouth can activate the vagus nerve, while circulating air throughout your respiratory system. This, in turn, activates parasympathetic nerves throughout your entire body, which reduces your heart rate and eases your body down into rest-and-digest mode.

Remember, however, that stress and anxiety are not just physical responses. These emotions are psychological responses, too, so their origin is not just external. A number of studies have connected self-criticism and low self-esteem to severe anxiety and depression. The more you beat yourself up, the more anxious you become as a person. A harsh inner voice and a low sense of self-worth can severely inhibit your ability to solve problems or tackle challenges. Anxiety often arises from a feeling of powerlessness or inability to adequately solve the problem at hand. More often than not, the belief that you aren't able to succeed comes from your self-esteem, not from an objective evaluation of your talents and abilities. If you don't believe you can succeed, then you probably won't, because instead of focusing all your energies into solving the problem at hand, your brain becomes overwhelmed with anxiety, self-hatred, and depression.

Therefore, another important strategy to cultivate a calm state of mind is to practice self-compassion. Don't be so critical of yourself. Nobody is perfect. Everyone makes mistakes. The problem is that our competitive modern society often leads us to believe that failure means we've done something wrong. Instead of learning from our mistakes in order to better ourselves, we see our mistakes as examples of why we're not good enough, smart enough, attractive enough, etc. We allow our mistakes to hold us back, when we should instead use them to propel ourselves forward toward success.

Affirmations are positive words and phrases that you repeat to yourself whenever you feel anxious or insecure. These affirmations are an extremely effective strategy to improve your sense of self-worth. Whenever you feel anxious, depressed, stressed, or frustrated, repeat your chosen affirmation to yourself in your mind, or even out loud. It can be anything, even something more general like "I can do this," something that will apply to almost any situation. You can also make specific affirmations for specific fears or stressors. For example, if you tend to be extremely self-critical about your physical appearance, your affirmation might sound something like "I will find one beautiful thing about myself every time I look in the mirror." The more you repeat your affirmation to yourself, the more you will start to believe it. Slowly but surely, the tone of your inner voice will start to change. Rather than self-criticizing, you will start to self-encourage, which will equip you with a mindset of confidence and resilience and greatly reduce the power of your stressors.

Chapter 7: Organization and Time are Key

No matter how busy or stressful your life may be, your system of organization and your schedule should be designed to best support you so that you can finish what needs to be done. If you constantly lose things, forget things, or show up late to commitments, then it's time to take a second look at how you structure your life. Chronic stress can shorten your attention span and make it difficult to focus, so your forgetfulness may be a symptom of stress. But no matter how well your system works for you, if you're constantly unable to function in times of stress, then that system needs to be adjusted. The extra stress of scrambling at the last minute is not something that you need in your life.

Organizing the Home

No matter where in your life your stressors originate, a cluttered living space can add to stress and anxiety levels. Clutter in the home can make it more difficult for your brain to focus, and therefore, more difficult for your body to relax - even if you consider the home to be a safe and comfortable space (Scott, 2019). Clutter in the home can also drain money from your budget and time from your schedule. This can take the form of lost or broken items, time spent hunting for important items like car keys and paperwork, or difficulty moving around easily in your own space. This, in turn, can create more stress in your finances or make it more difficult to successfully manage your time.

Organizing a home can feel like a formidable task, but there's no need to tackle your entire living space all at once. Instead, make a note in your stress journal every time you lose something, forget something, or show up late. Write down what it was that you lost or were late for, and the reason that it happened. For example, if you were late to work because you spent twenty minutes on the hunt for your keys, make a note of that. Where did you ultimately find your keys? Would it be valuable for you to have a designated key space? What room did you look for your keys in? If that room was less cluttered, would you have been able to find your keys more quickly? You may not have to re-organize your entire house - you may just need to reorganize the kitchen or hang a magnetic key-hook on your refrigerator. Focus on the small achievable things.

Time Management

Time management is essentially the art of organizing your time. If you constantly rush around, or show up late to places because you have way too much on your plate, then your schedule is in need of a second look. Many busy people feel that there is nothing they can do about how busy their schedule is. They have a lot to do, and they think they just have to roll up their sleeves and try their best to get everything done.

But the reality is that you have more control over your schedule than you realize. The first and most important rule of good time management is to not overschedule yourself. When you make a To-Do list, don't simply write down what you have to do, but also record how long it will take you to do it. Whether your task takes you five minutes or two hours, also schedule yourself an extra ten minutes for unexpected changes, interruptions, or challenges. If you have more items on your To-Do list than you have time to complete, determine if there are any items that you can eliminate, push to a later date, or delegate to someone else. You're not superhuman. If you try to push yourself to get more done than you have time for, you will only create more problems. Not only will it increase your stress levels, but it will decrease the quality of your work and your ability to focus.

If you don't already have a physical To-Do list, then it's time to make one! Whether it takes the form of a calendar, a notepad, or a spread-sheet - it doesn't matter. If you only keep all your tasks and commitments in your head, you will increase the likelihood to forget something important and cause yourself more stress. A written, physical To-Do list will help you prioritize tasks, and ensure that you get the most important items done first. Items that are less important you can either eliminate from your schedule entirely, roll over to an easier day, or delegate to someone else. It can be very difficult to determine which of your tasks are important if you spend all of your energy trying to remember everything that you have to do.

Finally, don't just schedule tasks like work, doctor's appointments, or meetings. Schedule yourself some downtime as well. No matter how much energy you have now, if you never give your mind and body a chance to rest, you will eventually start to burn out. It might seem like a waste to schedule yourself time to rest and relax everyday, but you will find that you are a lot more productive if you give yourself an adequate amount of time to rest, engage in self-care, or have personal time with a loved one.

Organization as Stress Management

Sometimes stressors are related to organization in ways that we don't even realize. For example, if you listed work as one of your major stressors because of your crowded commute, try to take a step back. When you sit in traffic and start to feel stressed, what causes that stress response? Almost always, people with stressful commutes are stressed because they do not want to be late for work. This common, work-related stressor is something that can be solved with organization. You can't change the amount of traffic on your commute, but can you leave the house a little earlier in the morning? If possible, talk to your boss about an adjustment to your work hours. Is it possible for you to start a bit later in the morning, and leave a bit later in the afternoon? Is it possible to do the opposite? Often, we have no control over certain stressors in our lives, but organization is something that we definitely have control over. Whenever you feel stressed, take a mental step back. Is there a way that you can adjust your schedule or your physical environment in order to eliminate this particular stressor?

The relationship between organization and stress isn't just about smoothing over logistics. Your brain constantly scans your physical environment and looks for signs of potential danger or other situations that might require some kind of energy investment on your part. If your surroundings are chaotic, your brain can sometimes decide that you are in danger, which then triggers the stress response (Voltolina, 2017). The same is true if your mindset is fragmented. If you constantly break your concentration to frantically find a paper that you misplaced, or remember the address of the doctor's office, then your brain registers this fractured mental energy as a sign that you're in a situation that requires more energy than you currently have (Voltolina, 2017). And if you perceive that you don't have enough resources to successfully navigate the situation in front of you, that triggers the stress response, too.

Getting yourself organized is also a way to feel like you're more in control of a situation, and the feeling of control is a great way to help your body relax. Even if you don't create an active solution to your stressors, make time to get yourself organized and eliminate the stress that comes from a cluttered space or an overbooked schedule. The act of organizing itself can even be considered a relaxation technique, because it helps to make your physical and mental environment more peaceful. Strange though it may sound, cleaning your room can help to relieve work-related stress. Organizing your desk can put you in a calm mindset so that you're ready to face the relationship stressors you may experience at home.

That being said, it's sometimes the case that our organization strategies are the very things that cause us to feel stress! Because of the sense of control they give us, we can sometimes become over-dependent on our organization strategies. This might be you if you constantly work from nine different To-Do lists, or check your digital calendar every minute. Organizational strategies should help us to feel calm and relaxed. If your organization technique causes you to feel more stress, then it doesn't work for you.

It's great to have a well-organized schedule. But if your schedule is too tightly packed, then even the slightest change or surprise can throw off your entire day. That can obviously create a great deal of stress, but what's even worse is that your brain will start to constantly worry about the possibility of change or surprise. Your schedule, in that case, may help you to stay organized, but it also fuels high levels of anxiety and makes it extremely difficult for you to handle change or challenges in a healthy way.

The best schedule is one that allows for a little bit of flexibility. Always give yourself that extra ten minutes for every item on your To-Do list, so that when the unexpected does happen, you have that buffer time to handle it, and can possibly reschedule the other items on your list. That little bit of scheduled "padding" can go a long way toward the relief of chronic anxiety, and help you to feel more confident in the face of challenge. And if you end up with a bit of extra time at the end of the day, that's an added bonus!

You can also choose to break big projects into smaller pieces. This essentially breaks one big, high-stress deadline into many smaller, low-stress deadlines. Look at one big project as a series of small pieces to help you to feel more relaxed and in control as the final deadline draws closer. Each time you complete a small piece of the project, you will feel more and more relaxed in the knowledge that the overall project will be finished on time. It also makes us feel good to complete a task, or to check an item off your To-Do list. Each time you complete a piece of your project, you'll enjoy the boost of confidence that inevitably comes with achieving goals.

Organization - A Three-Step Approach

Organization for stress management can easily be broken down into three simple steps. Remember, organization should only make you feel better, not cause you more stress. If the idea of a reorganization of your home, your schedule, or your workspace fills you with anxiety, then don't try to tackle the entire project all at once. Instead, follow these three stages to get yourself organized in a way that both calms and empowers.

Three-Step Organization

1. Schedule Your Organization Time

Set aside a designated time every day to plan and organize. I find that most people prefer to schedule their organization time in the morning, but if you prefer to work at night or in the middle of the day, that's okay, too. Tasks to be done during this time may include: make your To-Do List, fill out your schedule, clean your desk, check your emails, or throw away clutter. Whatever you need to do to get yourself planned and organized, do it during your set organization time. Just ten minutes of organization time a day can go a long way toward less stress and more control of your life.

That being said, make sure that you put a time limit on your organization time. If you set yourself ten minutes, then once those ten minutes are up, it's time to move on to the next thing on your schedule. The goal is to create daily habits, not finish in a single day. But also be sure that you don't allow yourself to be trapped in your planner. The more time you obsess over your schedule, the more stress you will feel, and the less time you will actually have to get things done. Ten minutes a day is all you need to get yourself planned, oriented, and organized.

2. Prioritize your Efforts

A general To-Do list item, such as "clean the house," is unlikely to be an effective organization strategy because "the house" is a big place. Unless you have an extra five hours to spare in your day, it will be way more efficient for you to organize more specific areas of your life that are cluttered or chaotic. One strategy is to dedicate a specific area of your life for each day's organization time. For example, imagine that you set your organization time for 1:15-1:30pm every day. On your calendar, dedicate Monday's organization time to simply organizing your inbox, Tuesday to only conquering the junk drawer, Wednesday to finalizing your filing cabinet, and so on. Instead of an attempt to organize your entire life all at once, you only need to spend 15 minutes a day to straighten out a specific area that needs some extra attention.

Alternatively, you can schedule an entire weeks' worth of organization time for one big area. Still 15 minutes a day, but tasks from Monday to Sunday cover the same area. Again, the idea is to create daily habits, not simply finish a task. So you might spend all of this week's 15 minute blocks on the task to "organize your desk," while next week you will organize a different area of your house. However you choose to do it, the idea is to focus on one area at a time. This will make the task of organization seem a lot more manageable. And as you start to reap the mental benefits of living an organized life, you might even find yourself looking forward to your organization time!

3. Eliminate Paper

Without a doubt, paper is the worst culprit when it comes to clutter. Mail, bills, receipts, and other paper documents can create quite a pile-up. It can be difficult to sort through what's important and what's not, and it can be difficult to efficiently store the paper documents that you determine are worth saving. Paper storage units like filing cabinets or desk drawers can also take up a lot of space, and can become cluttered and disorganized in their own right if they aren't carefully maintained or frequently cleaned out.

No matter how you feel about digital technology, it can often be easier to organize documents digitally than it is physically. The more paper you eliminate from your space, the easier it will be to keep yourself organized and decluttered. Certain apps like Genius Scan are free to download to your smartphone, helpful in this case, and easy to use. These apps help you to digitally scan everything from receipts to documents and store them in the appropriate files on your phone. If you don't use your phone for document storage, you can always email the files to yourself and store them on your computer. Either way, it eliminates the need for paper, reduces the likelihood that you'll lose or misplace an important paper, and reduces the amount of space you need for document storage. Unlike physical filing folders, files on your computer can hold thousands of documents without an increase in size, and will automatically sort themselves alphabetically by the name of the file.

We all tend to grow stacks of "stuff" around our houses, those piles of paper or other junk that we always say, "we'll get to later." The fewer stacks that collect around your home and office, the better you will feel. While files on your computer still need to be maintained and organized, it's much easier to periodically go through computer files than it is to go through physical filing cabinets or drawers. Digital file storage also relieves you of the burden of physically searching for important papers or documents. Wherever you have access to your phone or computer, you will have access to all of your important papers. And if you keep your computer well-organized, you'll never have to frantically hunt for the document that you need.

Chapter 8: Dealing with Stress in Real Life

No matter what your stressors are, the daily relaxation technique that you choose will help you to cultivate a calm state of mind so that your overall stress levels stay at a healthy and manageable level. However, if you experience chronic stress, then your body and brain have probably developed some automatic coping mechanisms, ones that aren't necessarily going to disappear when you start your relaxation practice. Unhealthy coping mechanisms are emotional habits. They're automatic and unconscious reactions that we experience when faced with certain situations. Slowly but surely, you can begin to retrain your brain away from these coping mechanisms. Everyone develops slightly different coping mechanisms to help them manage chronic stress, but there are certain coping mechanisms that are more common than others.

Anger

Perhaps the most common coping mechanism people develop when faced with stressful situations is anger. Whether you scream and honk at other drivers on the road or see red whenever your child refuses to listen, anger is not always something you can prevent or control. It's a feeling like any other, and when it wells up, trying to pretend that you don't feel as angry as you do will only lead to more problems.

Anger is essentially a fear response. It's the "fight" half of the "fight-or-flight" instinct our bodies experience when confronted with danger. So when the body enters the stress response, your temper becomes a lot shorter. When you're stressed, you become angry far more easily than you do when you're relaxed. While anger can be justified, and sometimes healthy when you are truly in a hostile situation, flying into a rage at home or snapping at your coworkers never makes a situation better. Instead, anger often causes us to lash out at others in ways that we regret later. Instead of protection from harm, anger often creates an even worse situation.

When you become angry, irritable, or even just frustrated, there are a few things you can do to calm yourself down and not allow your feelings to overwhelm you. The first and most important thing to do when you get angry is to *think before you speak*. Anger can make us say some pretty nasty comments in the heat of the moment, and cause serious damage to our relationships. Whenever you get angry, commit to taking one deep breath before you say anything out loud. Do this every time you're called to speak until you feel your anger start to recede. The few seconds it takes to take one deep breath can stop us from saying something that could potentially cause years of damage to a relationship. This technique also has the added benefit of more deep breathing, a tried-and-true relaxation technique for any situation (Mayo Clinic Staff, 2020, "Anger...").

Another important anger management step is to *name your feelings.* When you keep your anger under control like this you do not try to deny it or hide it. If you feel angry or irritated, tell the other person in a respectful and honest way. Express your feelings to someone else in a way that isn't hurtful or confrontational. Simply say to the other person, "It makes me angry when you say this," or, "I'm just tired right now and little things are annoying me. Can we talk about this tomorrow?" These statements can go a long way toward conflict management. Anger is a defense response, and so in the heat of the moment, it's hard to imagine that the other person might not realize how angry or frustrated you are. Name your feelings honestly and respectfully to help you and your partner communicate without a fight (Mayo Clinic Staff, 2020, "Anger...").

Remember that you are never obligated to remain in situations where you feel hurt, threatened, or unsafe. If you have a surge of anger, don't be afraid to *remove yourself from the situation.* Leave the room or the conversation and take a few minutes by yourself to cool down and think more clearly. It is extremely difficult to calm yourself down when you are in the midst of a conflict. The anger response was triggered within you because you felt unsafe, and it will be nearly impossible for you to release that anger while you still feel like you are under attack. Remove yourself from the situation to regain a sense of safety. If you then have to revisit the situation that made you feel angry, then you can do so from a calm and secure state of mind (Mayo Clinic Staff, 2020, "Anger...").

Dealing with Difficult People

No relationship is perfect. But some can be bad more often than they can be good. These relationships, whether with friends, family, or coworkers, can become strained or even toxic. You can recognize a strained relationship if you begin to dread spending time with someone or if you always seem to end up in conflict. In place of these, you need to cultivate more positive and supportive relationships as a necessary part of your health and wellbeing. The stress and emotional exhaustion of negative relationships can actually be detrimental to your physical health. The straightforward answer when faced with a difficult person is to minimize your contact with them as much as possible. But what do you do when the difficult person in your life is a family member, co-worker, or another person that you can't simply stop speaking to?

As much as possible, *keep conversations neutral* with people that you find difficult or a challenge to be around. Avoid topics that are extremely personal or important to you. Reserve those conversations for people who bring you joy, and the people that you really love to be around. With difficult people, try to stay away from topics that are extremely divisive, like religion or politics - especially if either one of you has strong opinions on the matter. You don't have to agree with everyone. To avoid a conversation that will lead to an unhelpful argument is not cowardice - it is simply common sense. If the other person tries to engage you in a sensitive conversation, don't be afraid to change the subject. If they persist or become aggressive with you, leave the conversation entirely. It is helpful to remain open to outside ideas, but you are in no way obligated to have a conversation that you know will distress you.

Perhaps one of the hardest aspects of dealing with a difficult person is needing to *accept them for who they are.* You can't change the other person, and there's never a situation in which it's acceptable to try. No matter how good or justified your intentions are, an attempt to force another person to be someone or something that they're not is not "support" - it creates a power struggle. The attempt to change another person will cause them instead to become defensive and feel criticized. It is very difficult to get someone to listen to you if they feel that you're overly critical. In this scenario, ultimately *you* have become the source of the conflict. If you don't like who or what someone is, try to ask them questions to help you better understand what makes them the way that they are. We all contain multitudes.

You are also never obligated to give up your power to someone else - *control what you can control.* You can't change someone else's behavior, but you can always change the way that you respond to that behavior. If someone does something that you don't like, speak up. You don't have to respond with anger or aggressiveness, but be firm. If someone has treated you in a way that makes you feel unhappy, let them know in a respectful and honest way. If they continue to behave in an unacceptable manner, remove yourself from the conversation.

No matter how unjustified another person's behavior may seem, the fact of the matter is that most difficult relationships are created by a toxic dynamic that occurs between two people. Unless you are in an abusive situation, there is probably something you could do differently to improve the quality of your relationship. Again, this comes down to an examination of the ways that you respond to the behavior of others. Whenever you find yourself engaged in conflict with a difficult person, take a mental step back. Is there something you could have done or said differently to avoid that conflict? The next time you are forced to spend time with this person, try to intentionally change the way that you respond to their difficult behavior. You may be surprised by how much a change in your reactions can improve the quality of your conversation. We sometimes don't realize how we come across to other people. You may unconsciously do something to make the other person feel hurt or defensive. While it never gives someone else the right to hurt or mistreat you back, it is important to take responsibility and at least make an effort to *create healthier patterns of communication* with this other person.

Something to keep in mind is that nobody in the world is completely "good" or completely "bad." When you engage with a difficult person, try to *focus on their positive qualities*. There is probably at least one quality about this other person that you can find to respect or admire. Focus on that one quality whenever you have to spend time with this person. Think about what you like about this other person instead of what you dislike and change the way that you engage with them. Your demeanor will be a lot less hostile. Almost always, the other person will respond positively to the change in your energy.

That being said, it is also important to *see the other person for who they are.* If you hate the fact that one of your friends can't keep a secret, then don't confide in them anymore. If your sibling constantly flakes out on you, then make less plans with them or rely on them for important commitments. Part of being able to accept someone for who they are is an acceptance of their negative traits. If someone is chronically unable to give you the affection you need, then it might be time to look for that affection elsewhere. Don't stubbornly try to force the other person to take on a role that you've assigned to them. That isn't fair to them or fair to you.

Assertive - To Be or Not to Be?

Assertiveness is a personality trait. Some people are naturally more assertive than others, and there's nothing immediately wrong with that. If you are a very assertive person, then you probably find it easy to fight for what you want. You may also be a straightforward communicator, unafraid of conflict, and find it easy to lay healthy boundaries in your relationships. However, not every situation calls for assertiveness. Sometimes being too assertive can create conflict, and that, in turn, creates stress. People might interpret your assertiveness as aggression, arrogance, or condescension. It's always good to be clear and honest about your needs and opinions. But depending on the social climate, it is sometimes advisable to let little things go or be a little more gentle.

Not every battle is worth the fight. Sometimes the people around us make mistakes. Sometimes people don't realize that they have hurt or inconvenienced us. Clear and honest communication is always good, but check your intensity. If you find it consistently difficult to get along with coworkers or constantly fight with your partner's family, take a mental step back. Is there a way that you could be a little more gentle or easygoing? Is there something about your communication style that causes the people around you to feel defensive or criticized?

On the other hand, not being assertive enough can also lead to stress. Not being able to clearly express or stand up for yourself can lead to a feeling of powerlessness and keep you from the things that you need out of life. People who are not naturally assertive tend to be more intuitive, gentle, and easygoing. You might find it easier to get along with people, and you may have good instincts when it comes to reading other people's feelings. Not being assertive certainly doesn't make you a pushover or a coward. Have you ever heard the saying, "You catch more flies with honey than with vinegar?"

Of course, certain people or situations in your life may sometimes call for a little vinegar. It is always okay to say "no" to requests that make you uncomfortable or to requests that will overburden you. It is also always okay to speak up if you feel angry or distressed. No one can read your mind. Often, others don't realize that the requests they make, or the way that they behave, causes you stress. The only way they will know is if you communicate clearly how you feel.

No matter what your situation may be, assertiveness is at the core of nearly every stressful situation. Whether in work, finances, or relationships, it is almost always a guarantee that if you feel stressed, then a state of assertiveness is part of the problem. Take a look at the situations in your life that stress you out. Are you too assertive in them, or are you not assertive enough? If you're not sure, it's okay to experiment. The next time you face a stressful situation, speak up. Lay stronger boundaries. Initiate conversations. See how the people around you react. Did your increase in assertiveness make the situation better? Or did it lead to more conflict?

Assertiveness is an especially important problem for people who experience stress in the workplace. Work-related stress is often interpersonal, even if it doesn't seem so on the surface. Even stressors such as low salaries, excessive workloads, or limited growth opportunities, are almost always rooted in how you interact with other people. If your salary is too low, have you asked for a raise? If your workload is more than you can handle, have you spoken to your boss or tried to delegate tasks out to other people? Are you saying "yes" to new assignments when you should be saying "no"? These situations might feel like they are totally out of your control, but it may really be the case that you are just not assertive enough. Asking for greater compensation for your role, or communicating to a superior that you feel overworked, are absolutely normal and acceptable parts of business communications. Any workplace that makes you feel like these ideas are not okay to say is not a healthy one. If you are underpaid or overworked (or both) and your boss doesn't want to acknowledge it, then it might be time to find another job.

However, work-related stressors can sometimes come from being a little *too* assertive. Your salary might be low, but are other people with your role paid a similar wage? It is always okay to negotiate for more money, but if your boss is not willing to increase your salary, it might not necessarily be because they undervalue you. If you already make a reasonable wage for your job and skill set, then a push for more money may create more stress and strain than it resolves. If you spend all of your energy on feelings of anger, or a sense of being undervalued, then you will further your stress and frustration. This can stop you from finding opportunities to increase your value in the workplace - and the option to argue for greater compensation in the future. No matter what causes you frustration at work, take a mental step back from the situation. Is this battle worth the fight? Is this situation worth the anger? Is there a way I can creatively solve this problem? Is this something that I simply need to let go of so that I can better enjoy other parts of my job and my life?

Chapter 9: Seven Examples of Stressful Events - Explained

Any situation can become a stressor depending on how you feel and react to it. However, there are seven major life events that are considered by psychologists to be the most likely to cause severe stress, both during, and long after an event has been resolved. Almost every individual will experience at least one of these events throughout their life, but it can be quite difficult to learn how to cope. Fortunately, there are many ways to handle the stress of these major events that are simple and grounding, ways that don't require much preparation or change to your already changing life.

Losing a Loved One

Perhaps the most stressful experience you can go through is the death of a loved one. Whether that person is a child, parent, family member, friend, or partner - grief is a very deep and often very traumatic experience. Everyone experiences grief differently. You may experience intense emotions like shock or anger. Other people experience feelings of guilt, depression, or even denial. While the intense feelings that come with grief are natural, they can later develop into trauma and long-term stress if they are not managed in a healthy way.

How to Manage the Stress of Losing a Loved One:

Perhaps the most important step you can take after losing a loved one is to *acknowledge your feelings*. Whether you feel shock, anger, or sadness, if you try to ignore or bury your feelings, it won't make them go away. If anything, it is the actual attempt to deny one's feelings that causes them to emerge later in life as chronic stress or deep-seated trauma. If you bottle up your feelings, you will place physical stress on the body, and create a great deal of psychological stress as you try to deny the truth of how you feel. If you have experienced the death of a loved one it is very important to be active and label your feelings, especially within the first three months. A mood chart is a useful tool to help name your feelings, and gives you more nuanced options than "good" or "bad," "happy" or "sad."

It is very important to accept that the emotions triggered by grief can be quite intense. Extreme emotions of anger or sadness are completely normal, and even healthy responses to grief. The loss of a loved one is a traumatic experience. Extreme emotions are your body's way of telling you that something terrible has happened. Acknowledging your feelings is a key part of this process. If you can acknowledge that you feel angry or depressed, then these surges of emotion won't take you by surprise. You won't be able to process your intense feelings in a healthy way if you can't even admit that you experience them. There is no shame in intense emotions, and there is no such thing as "too much" grieving, or an "overreaction" to the loss of a loved one.

Finally, remember that your grieving process will be unique to you. There is a common psychological grief scale developed in the 1960s called the Five Stages of Grief, which has helped many people to identify how they feel when faced with loss (Holland, 2018). The Five Stages of Grief are:

1. Denial
2. Anger
3. Bargaining
4. Depression
5. Acceptance

If in grief, use these five stages to better understand how you feel in the moment. Don't expect to move through the stages in the order that they are listed, and don't expect that you will experience every single stage. Everybody's grieving process is unique. Some people only experience two or three of the five stages. Some people experience depression before they experience anger, or even repeat stages that they have already experienced (Holland, 2018). There is no right or wrong way to grieve. The most important way to protect your body from even more stress is to know and accept where you are in the grieving process right now.

Major Illness or Injury

The diagnosis of a major illness or a severe injury can put much stress on the body. All of your body's resources will be devoted to healing the damage that has been done, whether that means fighting off an infection, managing a genetic condition, or repairing broken bones and tissues. Stress by itself can manifest as physical symptoms in the body, and so the stress sustained from a major illness or injury can make your experience much worse. Stress can prevent you from healing properly, cause you experience regressions, and put psychological problems on top of your physical ones.

How to Manage the Stress of Major Illness or Injury:

One of the biggest causes of stress that come from physical healing is uncertainty. Whether you've been diagnosed with an incurable condition or been in a severe car accident, what you will probably worry about most is the future. Will I be alright? Will I be able to return to my job or my passion? How will this affect my relationships? My family? The stress of not knowing what the future will hold is the most psychologically detrimental, one that can cause severe emotional distress if not managed in a healthy way. While there is no way to know the future for certain, *setting goals for therapy and rehabilitation* is a healthy way to plan for the future. Rather than a spiral down into endless worries about how to return to work or how much of a burden you will be on your partner, you can focus on the next step in your recovery. Set actionable goals for your recovery in order to give you something positive and productive to work toward. Enlist your family, friends, and doctors to help you to create and complete your recovery goals. This will also make you feel loved and cared for in a time that may be very painful or frightening, and will give your loved ones concrete ways in which they can support you.

If you focus on the outcome of your recovery goals, you will be better prepared to accept the changes that the illness or injury may make to your life. You can then adjust your lifestyle accordingly in small, actionable steps. Illness and injury can make us feel extremely powerless, and that powerlessness can also lead to extreme feelings of stress, fear, and anxiety. Focus on and achieve your recovery goals as a way to regain autonomy over your life. Complete these goals to fill you with much-needed confidence, and ensure that the additional physical symptoms of stress don't add to the pain you already experience.

Divorcing or Separating

Whether you need to divorce your married partner or separate from a long-term and intimate romantic partnership, the pain of separation can be so severe that many psychologists categorize it as a kind of grief. Your partner has not died, but in many ways you may feel as though you've lost them. You certainly may lose a relationship that once made you feel happy and secure. While they can also be positive experiences, often separations are angry or bitter, adding additional feelings of hurt, sadness, and pain to an experience that's already life-changing.

How to Manage the Stress of Divorcing or Separating:

View the end of your relationship as a loss that you need to grieve. Expect that you will experience a variety of intense emotions, and remember that these emotions are absolutely normal, common, and okay to feel. It doesn't matter if you have dated someone for three months or been married for ten years. There is no acceptable scale or timetable for the pain of separation, and, much like grief, there is no such thing as an "overreaction" to a separation. However, in the particular case of separation, the intensity of our feelings can sometimes lead us to do or say hurtful things to our former partner. Not only is this not a healthy way to process your own feelings, but it can make the situation between you and your ex-partner far more hostile. As such, *labeling your feelings* is an extremely important strategy for relieving stress and pain in a healthy way. This strategy is common to many stress management techniques, and we have written about this in a variation previously. If you try to ignore or dismiss your feelings, they can sometimes lead to an explosion outwards, which would cause you to do or say things that you would never normally do. All of your personal feelings are justified, but you cannot justify actions that are intentionally hurtful towards your partner. Even peaceful separations are painful. If you deny your feelings, you often make your situation worse. Name and accept the intensity of your emotions. Recognize them as a natural and healthy response to the pain of separation. Open, honest communication with your ex-partner is always a good idea, but during this process, don't try to confide or seek emotional support from them. This is a time instead to lean on the shoulder of a good friend or family member.

It is also important to be gentle with yourself during and immediately after the separation. Don't expect that you will perform as well at your job or keep up as efficiently with your household duties. Give yourself permission to take a break, and give yourself the space you need to heal from your loss. If you need some time to be alone, take it. If you need help to meet a deadline or complete a task that you would normally have been able to handle by yourself, don't be afraid to ask your loved ones for support. Remember that your ex-partner was not the only meaningful connection in your life. Reach out to family, friends, and even coworkers for a little extra support during your grieving period.

Financial Difficulties

Whether you experience a sudden loss of income or incur new major expenses like student loans, medical bills, or an increase in rent - financial difficulties can be an extreme source of stress. Concerns about the money that you need to pay your bills and support yourself can have serious consequences for your health. That stress only increases if other people are dependent on you for their security. Financial distress is increasingly common, and will soon become the number one cause of stress in the United States today. You are not alone.

How to Manage the Stress of Financial Difficulties:

Finances rarely affect just one area of your life. Your bills could cover: rent or mortgage, credit cards, medical, food, utilities, or even transportation. These often directly relate to your feelings of security in the home, as is the case with rent and utilities. If you have to scramble to pay one bill, it can often lead to a slippery slope of quick fixes and bad financial coping strategies that cause you even more stress and financial troubles down the road. The best way to cope with the stress that comes from financial strain is to *make one financial decision at a time*. Another way to think about this is to find one solution at a time. Don't all at once try to work more hours at your current job, take on a second (or third) job, ask your parents for help, and take out a new credit card. Don't make multiple changes to your finances all at one time, either. If you try to pay off your credit cards, save for retirement, and put your kids through college all at the same time, you will be left completely overwhelmed. Make one major financial goal your primary focus, and then manage the rest.

I understand that when you feel like you're drowning, this can be difficult advice to follow. But if you choose to focus on one item at a time, it will improve your ability to problem-solve. Instead of a constant scramble between items, make one financial goal your top priority. This will relieve stress and prevent you from making sudden, impulsive decisions out of fear or desperation. Determine what your number one financial priority is. Is it making enough to pay rent? Paying off your credit card debt? Getting ahead of your mortgage? Whatever it is, focus all of your efforts on solving that single problem. If paying off your mortgage is your most important goal, reorient your budget and financial habits around it. Pay the minimums on other bills like credit cards. Invest the minimum amount into your retirement fund or savings account. Tackle the most important problem first, and afterwards, you will find it easier to tackle your other financial prospects.

Losing a Job

Losing a job can be stressful for financial reasons, but it can also be a source of extreme emotional distress. Losing a job can lead to feelings of rejection, inadequacy, and low self-esteem. Regardless of the reason, many people feel shame, worthlessness, or even guilt after losing a job, especially if someone else is dependent on them. This can create some obvious financial stress, but it can also create stress in terms of our identities and social wellbeing. For many people, what they do for work is an important part of their identity, and so losing a job can negatively impact the way that they see themselves. Jobs can also be important social outlets, ones that might be cut-off or damaged.

How to Manage the Stress of Losing a Job:

No matter how you feel about your job, losing it will always be difficult. Not only have you lost a source of financial stability, but you have also potentially lost a feeling of control over your life, a professional identity, and self-esteem. Your self-confidence may take a hit, and your daily routine is greatly affected, leaving you with empty hours in your day. If your job was a social outlet or if one of your coworkers developed into a real friend, then you may also experience a loss of meaningful social connections. Perhaps most significantly, losing a job means a loss of security, for you and for your family.

So treat it as a proper loss, and *allow yourself to grieve*. Treat the loss of your job the same way that you would treat any other kind of loss. Accept the intensity of your feelings. Be proactive and label your emotions. Understand that strong feelings are completely normal. Reach out to your loved ones for emotional support, and be honest about your emotional needs. Most importantly, don't put pressure on yourself to go out and get a new job right away. This can be difficult advice to follow, especially if you face extreme financial pressure. But if you insist to yourself that you have to get another job as soon as possible, you will put an enormous amount of additional stress on yourself that you don't need. You are already under a lot of stress. Give yourself a few days to grieve, and when you jump back into the professional marketplace, put healthy limits on the amount of time and effort you put into the job search.

Having a Child

A new baby can be a great joy. However, a child can also be an extreme source of stress. A child represents new responsibilities, a number of different lifestyle changes, and new financial concerns. It is a lot of work to care for a child, and even when you're away, it will still be on your mind. Many people try to hide or downplay the stress they feel after the birth of a new child because of a feeling of shame or embarrassment. But that stress does not make you a bad or unloving parent. It is perfectly normal, common, and natural to feel overwhelmed by the responsibilities of a new life, no matter how many children you may already have.

How to Manage the Stress of Having a Child:

There are many different reasons why the arrival of a new child can be stressful, but one of the biggest sources of stress actually comes from the change in routine. The presence of a new member in your household radically changes your daily routine. There is suddenly a lot more that has to be done, and you probably feel as though you have less time to do it all. Worse, these new items are pushed to the top of your list. You can't reschedule or delegate your child, and often, you can't predict what your child will need from day to day. While you scramble to find a way to efficiently manage your time, it is very important to *set aside time for yourself.* Many parents find that the best time for this is just after the child (or children) have gone to sleep, but you can schedule this at any time that works for you and your family. Give yourself an hour every day to do something that you enjoy: take a bath, read a book, or watch TV. The amount of energy and time required to be a new parent makes relaxation time and self-care extra important. Without it, you will quickly burn out, and your stress symptoms will get worse and worse. If an hour for yourself means putting off housework or social obligations, then so be it. At this point in your life, taking care of yourself is just as important as taking care of your new baby. You need to be balanced in order to best help the others that rely on you.

Retirement

Believe it or not, retirement can be one of the most stressful events a person will experience in their lifetime. Many people spend the second half of their lives dreaming about their retirement, but are totally unprepared for the stress that accompanies it. This doesn't mean that your retirement will not be as wonderful as you planned. But retirement is a major life change, and like all major life changes, it comes with a fair amount of stress. What makes retirement particularly stressful is often the lack of preparation for that change.

How to Manage the Stress of Retirement:

One of the main reasons that retirement is so stressful is the change it makes to your identity. For many people, their career plays a major role in how they define themselves and how they relate to others. A job can define that part of yourself and how you live your life for decades. When that suddenly ends, it can create a kind of identity crisis. As a new retiree, you now have to rethink who you are and how you want to live your life. While that can be an exciting opportunity, it can also be extremely frightening. The best way to avoid this sudden crisis of identity is to *retire slowly*. In the years before you plan to officially retire, try to reduce your hours or work part-time. This will give you more time to plan your life post-retirement, while simultaneously relieving the stress that comes with a 40 hour workweek. After a year or two of a reduced schedule, you will be comfortable and secure enough to officially end your career and start your new life as a relaxed retiree.

A slow retirement also gives you time to put your finances in order. Saving for retirement is something that most people only start to think about in middle age, so that they have enough to live on when they leave work. However, financial stability can be difficult (and stressful) to maintain even when you are at the peak of your career. Even the best planners can find themselves with unforeseen costs as retirement looms closer. Don't wait until retirement to learn that you don't have enough to cover your medical bills, or to live your preferred comfortable life. Instead, take the year or two prior to focus and go over your finances. You can then determine what adjustments will need to be made to ensure your financial security when you officially leave work.

Chapter 10: The Seven Habits of Good Stress Managers - Explained

All of the advice, techniques, and suggestions offered in this book can be grouped into seven major categories. Remember, these habits all take time to form, so don't expect to master them overnight. However, if you introduce any of these habits into your daily life, you will not only decrease your future stress levels, but you will also help your body to recover and heal from the damage done by living with stress in the past.

Knowing How to Relax

Your daily relaxation time may only be 5-15 minutes, but it will help you to feel calm and relaxed for hours afterward. Relaxation sounds like something you should be able to do automatically, but it is actually a habit you need to learn. It is something that you need to learn and practice every day, and it will take some time before it starts to feel comfortable or natural. According to a Wall Street Journal study, about 25% of their participants could be classified as workaholics, and 3% of their participants actually reported feeling physically ill when they tried to relax on vacation (Pinola, 2014). Our reactions to stress are learned habits as well, and it will take some time for you to unlearn those - in order to replace them with what your body and mind need to fully unwind.

Use your stress journal to help teach yourself what works for you and what doesn't. Take time to reflect on your relaxation techniques, record your stress levels every day, and keep track of your stressors. Whatever you determined your major stressors to be at the beginning of this book should be your main focus. Employ any strategy you can to relieve stress from those areas of your life. Make a note of how you feel in special situations or with people that stress you out. Return to those notes after you start your daily relaxation practice. Do you notice a change in your stress levels? Are you finding solutions to problems that you once thought were inevitable or unavoidable?

There is no one right or wrong way to relax. Some people find a great deal of stress relief from yoga, but it makes other people feel self-conscious, tired, or frustrated. Many people prefer the mental health benefits of meditation, but many others struggle with the practice. The key isn't just to relax, it is to know what works for you. If something causes difficulty for you, then don't feel obligated to keep at it. You should spend as much time thinking about your unique relaxation signature as you do your unique stress signature. We learned about stress signatures back in Chapter 3 - what are your stressors and what are your symptoms. Now, what kinds of situations, stimuli, or actions will make you feel relaxed? The more specifically you can answer that question, the better you will build your relaxation habit. Ultimately, it will become strong enough to counter your stress habits.

Eating and Exercising Correctly

It can't be overstated just how beneficial healthy eating and regular exercise is for the body. More nerves connect your brain to your gut than to any other organ in the body. The food that you eat affects everything from your energy levels to your mood to your body's ability to fight off disease. Thousands of studies have shown how healthy eating and exercise can be even more effective than prescription drugs to treat everything from cancer to diabetes to stress. You could consider an unbalanced diet a stressor simply because of the negative ways that it affects the body.

So, what does it actually mean to eat and exercise "correctly?" Should you go on a special diet? Should you count calories? What kind of exercises are best? There is so much information out there that it is difficult to know what works best for, especially when much of that information is conflicting. The best thing to do, always, is to listen to your body. If less carbs makes you feel better, then eat less and find substitutes. But if cutting carbs makes you sick, then keep incorporating them into your diet. Only you can know what routine works best for you, but I find that there is one single, simple dietary change with the greatest benefit and stress management impact.

Eat breakfast. Not necessarily a huge breakfast. But it is important to have something within a few hours of waking up. Many people count morning coffee as breakfast, but while coffee can give your brain a bit of a boost, it doesn't nourish your body with the nutrients it needs to thrive. On the other hand, many people also choose sweet or fatty comfort foods in the morning, like pancakes, bacon and eggs, or pastries. While these foods are tasty, they are also loaded with trans fats and sugars, which can even be worse than eating nothing at all. Whole-grain cereals, bread, low-fat milk, juice, a banana, yogurt, or pancakes are all great breakfast options. These options provide you with macronutrients (carbs, proteins, and healthy fats) that give your body the energy it needs to get you going in the morning. These meals are also packed with micronutrients, which are the vitamins and minerals that provide your body with nutrition.

Sleep Well and Enough

Sleep problems plague people who deal with chronic stress. Insomnia is a very common stress symptom, but insomnia itself can be a stressor, sending those with sleep problems into a vicious cycle of stress-related insomnia and insomnia-related stress. It is recommended that you get between seven and nine hours of sleep every night, but some people need a little less and others need a little more. But where many people get stuck is not the amount of time they spend asleep, but the quality of the sleep itself. Laying in your bed staring at the ceiling for seven hours is not the same as a full-night's sleep. Your sleep quality diminishes if you toss and turn, wake up repeatedly, or experience night terrors. Even if you manage to stay asleep for a full eight hours, if the overall quality of that sleep wasn't good, then it can still contribute to health problems in the brain and body.

A daily relaxation habit will naturally improve the quality of your sleep. If you're someone who struggles with insomnia, then you may want to consider a schedule with relaxation time just before you go to bed. But no matter when you've chosen to build your relaxation habit, it is always important to be screen-free for at least fifteen minutes before you go to bed. Smartphones, tablets, laptops, and TVs all emit a shade of blue light that stimulates the brain. Your eyes may begin to droop while you scroll through your smartphone before bed, but the stimulation to your brain can make it difficult for you to fall into a deep, restful sleep. It is also advised not to do anything in your bed except sleep. Your meals, your work, and your TV habits should be kept in another room. When you get into your bed, you want your brain to automatically start to prepare for sleep. If your bed is a place where you engage in many stimulating activities, then it can become difficult for your brain and body to relax while you're there.

Managing Anger

After anxiety, anger is the most commonly experienced symptom of stress. Feelings of irritability, frustration, and rage can be extremely difficult to control, and can rise up at even the slightest provocation. Too often, we unleash our anger on other people in an attempt to release some of the emotional pressure that stress builds up inside us. Unfortunately, this almost always makes the situation worse, adds damaged personal relationships to your list of stressors, and makes your anger even more difficult to manage.

A great anger-management strategy is the use of "I" statements. It can be far too easy to lay blame and hurl hurtful words at others when we feel angry. If we use "I" statements, we instead produce more constructive comments and communicate our feelings in a clear and respectful way. Of course, not all anger is unwarranted. If someone says something hurtful or acts violently, anger is a normal and occasionally helpful response. But no matter how justified our anger may be, it is still not okay to be hurtful or violent ourselves.

"I" statements are exactly what they sound like - statements that start with "I." Instead of saying something unhelpful ("You're so lazy, you never do anything to help around the house") try something more constructive ("I am upset that you left the table without offering to do the dishes"). Your "I" statement can take as many forms as you have feelings ("I feel really frustrated when you leave your dishes in the sink for me to clean"). Instead of laying blame and judgment on someone else, keep the conversation focused on you and your feelings. Another powerful anger management strategy is empathy. If you find yourself in continuous conflict with the same person, try to imagine what is going on in their life. Why do they behave that way? Try to imagine how they feel when you shout or speak sarcastically. If you imagine the other person's perspective, it can help you to let go of your anger and lead you to positive solutions that you were not able to see during the conflict.

Time Organization

There is nothing more overwhelming than a busy schedule. The feeling of having too much to do can be a significant source of stress. If we juggle too many commitments, we often make mistakes or miss important details that leave us with even *more* work to do, which increases our stress even more. If you feel stressed, then it is critically important to take a look at how you manage your time. Most people with busy schedules say that there is nothing they can do, but if you give yourself a moment to pause, you will find that there is almost always a way to give yourself a little bit of time to breathe.

A very important factor of good time management is to set clear goals. Often, individuals are overwhelmed with commitments because they don't have a clear vision of what they want out of life. It is difficult to make positive lifestyle decisions without being sure of what kind of life you want to lead, or even worse, when you try to follow goals that have been given to you by someone else. If you ever feel totally overwhelmed, take a moment to answer this question in your stress journal: *If I could magically change one thing about my life, with just a snap of my fingers, what would it be?* The answer to that question will almost always be a major source of stress for you. Now take a look at your life. Is there anything that you can do to make that change a reality? You may not be able to snap your fingers and make your supervisor or your debt disappear, but there is probably something you can change to make those stressors less potent. If you have a bad relationship with your supervisor, maybe dedicate some time in the morning to look for a new job. Arrive at the office earlier so that you can get settled before they arrive. If you're swamped with debt, make it your primary goal to pay it off. Once you focus your attention on the achievement of one purpose, you will suddenly find it much easier to make positive time management decisions. When paying off debt becomes a goal rather than a wish, you'll find it much easier to say "no" to situations that would increase the debt, or make it more difficult to pay off. You might also find it easier to take on greater financial opportunities, or find more motivation at your current job. With a goal to work toward, it will be much easier for you to eliminate unnecessary obligations from your schedule. You will find yourself with more energy to complete the tasks that move you toward the achievement of your goal.

Filter Out the Unimportant Things

The more stress something causes us, the more we start to magnify its importance in our lives. In the grand scheme of your life, your job might just be an easy way to pay the bills. But if you feel overworked or find yourself in constant conflict with your coworkers, then your job will start to feel like it is taking over your life. Rather than put your effort into the opportunities that *are* important to you, you will find yourself consumed with a job that was never meant to be the center of your life.

Keep your stressors in perspective as an effective way to manage how much they bother you. If something or someone is not that important to you, then don't waste your valuable time and energy on it. Instead, pour that energy and time into the things that are valuable to you. Identify the most important people in your life, and put all of your efforts into the maintenance of those positive relationships. If your boss, or your mother-in-law, or your ex-boyfriend are not on that list of important people, then choose not to let them get to you. Find ways to keep conversation civil when difficult people are around, but don't waste your time and struggle to make it work when instead you could spend time with someone that you truly love.

Take a look at your skills and talents. What you're naturally good at often contains clues about what you truly value, or the situations that make you naturally feel secure. If you're really good at something obscure like marbles or ping pong, try to think about *why* you're so good at those games. Are you naturally dexterous? Do you enjoy healthy competition? Maybe you enjoy fine skill over brute force? This won't necessarily mean that you are destined to become a professional ping pong player, but whatever makes you successful at ping pong may also be a skill you can take to other parts of your life. It is healthy to seek things out that you are good at. You will feel more confident, and therefore more relaxed, if you seek out situations that allow your natural gifts to thrive.

Try Having Humor

Laughter truly is the best medicine. The ability to make people laugh will naturally make people feel more relaxed around you, and in turn, make you feel relaxed about them. If you can find the humor in a situation, no matter how stressful, then that will make it much more manageable. Laughter is also a natural way to release tension, and a much healthier method than anger.

Finding the humor doesn't mean you will make light of a serious situation. It is just a way to keep things in perspective, and to help you face life with joy rather than tension.

Humor is a communication skill, and it is one that doesn't always come easy. Everyone has a slightly different sense of humor, and your sense of humor can even change slightly depending on who you're with. Not every situation is a laughing matter, and making a joke about a topic that the other person feels is insensitive can create greater tension, rather than diffusing it. Not everyone finds silly or raunchy humor amusing, and it is very easy to mishear sarcasm, especially if it comes from a stranger.

It can be complicated to keep all this in mind and make humor seem like a pretty risky endeavor, or even take the fun out of it. But don't let it stress you out. Humor should lessen your stress, not add to it. The trick with humor is not to worry about doing something silly or having a perfect clever quip. Instead, just think about ways to make the person in front of you smile! Laughter doesn't have to come from jokes or humor. It can come from something sweet, or pleasantly surprising. Make it your goal to make the person you're with smile, and you will almost certainly get a laugh from them as a bonus. Think about what will make the other person smile to help take your mind off of your own stress or feelings of awkwardness. It will help you to connect with that person on a closer level. And, of course, it always feels good to make someone else happy. Making other people smile and laugh is an almost instant stress reliever.

Conclusion

Every individual will experience stress at one point in their lives. That's honest, and that's okay. A little bit of stress can actually be good for us. It can give us an extra boost of energy when we lack motivation, or make us aware of problems that we couldn't see before. Stress is built into our bodies as a natural response to danger. In many ways, stress is what keeps us alive. It alerts us to threats, and provides us with the energy and alertness that we need to successfully combat them.

However, when stress becomes chronic, then our bodies and minds are thrown out of balance. Just as we need a little bit of stress to thrive, we also need to relax. Without time to rest and recuperate from the stresses of life, our bodies become physically weakened and even ill. Our minds stop working as effectively. We find it more and more difficult to think clearly, regulate our moods, and even start to develop harmful psychological patterns or disorders.

You chose to read this book because you felt the harmful presence of chronic stress in your life. No matter how long you battled stress in the past, or how severe your stressors are, you now have all the tools you need to manage your stress in a healthy way that works uniquely for you. No two people's stress is identical. But you now have a clear understanding of what your stressors are and how they affect your body and mind. To understand your stressors is half the battle. With your stress journal in hand, you are now ready to take action to get your stress back under control.

Perhaps the most important technique outlined in this book is to schedule a daily relaxation time. Spend just five minutes a day on a deep breathing technique and watch it work wonders for your mental and physical health. Build from there. Don't reject a technique out of hand because it sounds simple. Stressful situations are often big and complex, and so we tend to feel that our solutions should be big and complex as well. But stress is the opposite of relaxation, in almost every way. It is often the case that the simplest of relaxation techniques has the greatest effect on the most complex life stressors.

As you start to apply the techniques outlined in this book, always remember to be patient with yourself. No technique will work immediately. Remember, stress is a habit too. Our stress responses often surprise us; they take over our thoughts and behaviors before we even realize what happened. The management of those automatic thoughts and feelings will take some time and practice. It may take you a while to find a relaxation technique that works well for you. You may also learn new sides to your stressors and your responses to them. Why do they stress you out the way they do? You might even realize that what you initially thought was a stressor was really just a distraction, and that there is another, truer source of stress to tackle. The more you learn about yourself, the more effective action you can take to manage your stress. You may even find yourself with the tools to eliminate your stressors altogether.

Stress has a unique ability to distort our situation, and make it look much worse than it actually is. No matter how terrible you feel, know that there is always something you can do to make the situation better. But before you can start to find a solution, you have to find a way to relax. We are naturally better problem-solvers when we're relaxed, as opposed to when we're stressed. Stress management can be a cure, but it can also be a prevention strategy. A daily relaxation habit is intended to help you feel relaxed all the time. Don't wait for moments of stress to practice your relaxation techniques. While there are many strategies in this book that you can employ in the moment to help you through a bad situation, these situational coping strategies are no match for a daily relaxation habit. Right now, your mind's natural state may be one of stress. Your automatic responses to new situations may be fear, anger, and frustration. But as you start to practice your daily relaxation technique, you will start to feel your perspective shift. Rather than fear or anxiety in new situations, you will instead find feelings of excitement, wonder, and curiosity. Rather than a rage response, you will instead calmly roll up your sleeves and resolve the sudden changes or challenges in front of you.

My hope for you is that, where once you felt overwhelmed, you now feel empowerment. You now have the tools you need to take back control of your mind, your feelings, and your life. And above all, you now have the ability now to feel good about yourself. I know that with time and patience, you will find relaxation techniques that work for you. Once you do - your life will transform for the better. You already took a huge first step by simply reading this book, so good luck on your journey! Know that there is at least one person out there rooting for you!

References

Albrecht, Karl. (1979). *Stress and the Manager.* New York, York: Simon & Schuster.

Avoiding Roadblocks to Stress Reduction. (2016, March 26). https://www.dummies.com/religion/spirituality/avoiding-roadblocks-to-stress-reduction/

Butler, G. (1993, August 1). Definitions of Stress. https://www.ncbi.nlm.nih.gov/pmc/articles/PMC2560943/

Davis, M., Eshelman, E. R., & McKay, M. (2008). *The Relaxation and Stress Reduction Workbook.* New York, New York: New Harbinger Publications.

Elkin, A. (2013). *Stress Management For Dummies.* Hoboken, NJ, United States: Wiley.

Figueroa-Frankhanel, Frances. (2014, December 12). Measurement of Stress. https://secure.jbs.elsevierhealth.com/action/cookieAbsent?code=null

Freeman L (2009). Relaxation therapy. In Mosby's Complementary and Alternative Medicine: A Research-Based Approach, 3rd ed., pp. 129–157. St. Louis: Mosby Elsevier.

Haas, S. (2017, September 30). 7 Ways to Calm Your Worried Mind and Reduce Anxiety.
https://www.psychologytoday.com/us/blog/prescriptions-life/201709/7-ways-calm-your-worried-mind-and-reduce-anxiety

Holland, K. (2018, September 25). What You Should Know About the Stages of Grief.
https://www.healthline.com/health/stages-of-grief

Kunos, G., and Ciriello, J. (1992). *Central Neural Mechanisms in Cardiovascular Regulation, Vol. 2.* Boston, Birkhauser.

Lazarus, R.S., and Folkman, S. (1984). *Stress, Appraisal and Coping.* New York, Springer.

Lazarus, R.S., and Holroyd K.A. (1982). *Stress, Coping and Somatic Adaptation.* New York, Springer.

Legg, Timothy. (2020, March 29). Causes of Stress: Recognizing and Managing Your Stressors.
https://www.healthline.com/health/stress-causes

Manage Your Stress: A Three-Pronged Approach. (2016, March 26).
https://www.dummies.com/health/mental-health/stress-management/manage-your-stress-a-three-pronged-approach/

Mayo Clinic Staff. (2020, February 29). Anger Management: 10 Tips to Tame Your Anger. https://www.mayoclinic.org/healthy-lifestyle/adult-health/in-depth/anger-management/art-20045434

Mayo Clinic Staff. (2020, April 18). Relaxation Techniques: Try These Steps to Reduce Stress. https://www.mayoclinic.org/healthy-lifestyle/stress-management/in-depth/relaxation-technique/art-20045368

NHS Inform. (2020, April 24). Relaxation Techniques. https://www.nhsinform.scot/healthy-living/preventing-falls/fear-and-anxiety-about-falling/relaxation-techniques

Pinola, M. (2014, March 20). How You Can Learn to Finally, Really Relax. https://lifehacker.com/how-you-can-learn-to-finally-really-relax-1548045887

Puddicombe, A. (2011, January 24). How to meditate in 10 easy steps. https://www.theguardian.com/lifeandstyle/gallery/2011/jan/22/how-to-meditate-ten-steps-headspace

Scott, E. (2019, June 24). How to Get Organized to Manage Stress. https://www.verywellmind.com/tips-on-getting-organized-3145158

Scott, E. (2020, January 19). The Main Causes of Stress. https://www.verywellmind.com/what-are-the-main-causes-of-stress-3145063

Segal, J., Smith, M., Segal, R., and Robinson, L. (2020, April 16). Stress Symptoms, Signs, and Causes. https://www.helpguide.org/articles/stress/stress-symptoms-signs-and-causes.htm

Selye, H. (1956). *The Stress of Life*. New York, McGraw-Hill.

Seppala, Emma. (2019, November 7). Four Ways to Calm Your Mind in Stressful Times. https://greatergood.berkeley.edu/article/item/four_ways_to_calm_your_mind_in_stressful_times

Stress Definitions from Stress Researchers. (2013, March 31). http://www.gostress.com/stress-definitions-from-stress-researchers/

Voltolina, V. (2017, September 22). 3 Easy Tricks to Get Organized and Reduce Stress. https://www.huffpost.com/entry/organization-and-stress_n_5851704?guccounter=1&guce_referrer=aHR0cHM6Ly93d3cuZ29vZ2xlLmNvbS8&guce_referrer_sig=AQAAAJwZSkH65kL_I4oait4Okd1wfo59-2sOzBBVGJYQHo1iX2y9Hdx-gUONVDmi1tp3FM8xV4RzZn-wwP9jlXDioXGXWltiz1BEatmSmCjSj3Hat-fbJEm48p-Xp6573f5JJSzpwvjUoOvp47Yzp2ldngPjpOYTW2ffuV3ohwQwemBo

Printed in Great Britain
by Amazon

62942558R00149